Environmental Law in Mexico

Second Edition

Jose Juan Gonzalez Márquez

This book was originally published as a monograph in the International Encyclopaedia of Laws/Environmental Law.

Founding Editor: Roger Blanpain
General Editor: Frank Hendrickx
Volume Editor: Kurt Deketelaere

Wolters Kluwer

Published by:
Kluwer Law International B.V.
PO Box 316
2400 AH Alphen aan den Rijn
The Netherlands
Website: www.wolterskluwerlr.com

Sold and distributed in North, Central and South America by:
Wolters Kluwer Legal & Regulatory U.S.
7201 McKinney Circle
Frederick, MD 21704
United States of America
Email: customer.service@wolterskluwer.com

Sold and distributed in all other countries by:
Quadrant
Rockwood House
Haywards Heath
West Sussex
RH16 3DH
United Kingdom
Email: international-customerservice@wolterskluwer.com

ISBN 978-90-411-9228-8

e-Book: ISBN 978-90-411-9263-9
web-PDF: ISBN 978-90-411-9295-0

This title is available on www.kluwerlawonline.com

The Author

Jose Juan Gonzalez Márquez (b. 1959), who holds a Juris Doctor Degree (Mexico, 1981), an LLM in Economic Law (Mexico, 1984) and a PhD in Environmental Law (Spain, 1999) is a full Professor and Researcher at the Metropolitan Autonomous University in Mexico and head of the Environmental Law PhD Programme administered by the Metropolitan Autonomous University in cooperation with the University of Alicante, Spain. In addition to his research and scientific service, he teaches the courses Property of Natural Resources, Tax Law, and Environmental Law. He is also the chairman of the Mexican Institute for Environmental Law Research and Director of the *Mexican Environmental Law Journal.* Gonzalez is a fellow of the National Research System of the Mexican Council of Science and Technology. He was also member of the Governing Council of the UICN Academy of Environmental Law during the period 2005–2013 and of the Academic Advisory Group of the International Bar Association, Energy Section, Environment and Infrastructure Law.

In the past, he was Director of the Legal Division of the Attorney General's Office for Environmental Protection.

Gonzalez is the author of several books and articles in the field of Latin American and Mexican Environmental Law, Tax Law, and Energy Law. Besides his academic activities, he is adviser for a number of Federal and local governmental agencies in the field of environmental enforcement and compliance. In 1999, he drafted the currently in force Environmental Act of Mexico City.

Gonzalez is also a member of the editorial boards of the *Energy and Natural Resources Law Journal* and the *Macquarie Journal of International and Comparative Environmental Law.* In 2008, he organized the Sixth Annual Colloquium of the UICN Academy of Environmental Law.

The Author

Table of Contents

Table of Contents

List of Abbreviations

Agencies

AIE	International Agency of Energy
CONAPO	National Council of Population
Environmental Prosecutor	Attorney General's Office for Environmental Protection
Ministry of the Environment	Secretary of the Environment and Natural Resources
PEMEX	Mexican Petroleum Company
SCJN	National Supreme Court of Justice
SEMARNAP	Secretary of the Environment, Natural Resources, and Fishing

Legislation

AA	Agrarian Act
Access to Information Act	Federal Act of Transparency and Access to Information
ASRD	Act for Sustainable Rural Development
Civil Code	Civil Code of the Federal District as Regards the Common Jurisdiction and for the Whole Republic as Regards the Federal Jurisdiction
Environmental Act	Ecological Equilibrium and Environmental Protection General Act
FAAP	Federal Act of Administrative Procedure
FAD	Federal Act of Duties
FAS	Federal Act of the Sea
Fishing Act	General Act for Sustainable Fishing and Aquaculture
Forest Act	General Act for Sustainable Forest Development
GASFA	General Act of Sustainable Fishing and Aquaculture

LGEEPA	General Law of Ecological Equilibrium and Environmental Protection
MA	Mining Act
Mexican Constitution	Constitution of the Mexican United States
MNs	Mexican Norms
OMNs	Official Mexican Norms
NWA	National Water Act
RACNM	Regulatory Act of Article 27 of the Constitution on Nuclear Matters
RACOB	Regulatory Act of the Constitution on the Oil Branch
REEEPGAPCAP	Regulation under EEEPGA in the Field of Prevention and Control of Air Pollution 1988
	Regulation under EEEPGA in the Field of Prevention and Control of the Pollution Originated by the Emission of Fumes and Powders
Regulation of Marine Water Pollution	Regulation under the Convention on the Prevention of Marine Pollution by Dumping of Wastes and Other Matters
Regulation on EIA	Regulation under EEEPGA in Regard to Environmental Impact Assessment
Standardization Act	Federal Act of Metrology and Standardization
TENs	Technical Official Norms
Urban Act	General Act of Human Settlements
Waste Act	General Act of Prevention and Integral Management of Waste
Wildlife Act	General Act of Wildlife

General Introduction

§1. General Background

I. Geography and Population

A. Geography

1. Mexico is located in the North American Continent. Its official name is United Mexican States. The country has a territory of 1,972,547 km^2, placing it fourteenth in geographical size among all countries.

2. In the north, the Mexican Republic has a border of 3,152 km with the United States of America; to the south, it borders Guatemala and Belize along 956 km and 193 km, respectively.

3. Its geographic position has favoured Mexico. It is located between two great oceans that bathe its coasts, 70% of which border the Pacific Ocean and 30% of which borders the Gulf of Mexico and the Sea of the Antilles.

4. The main rivers crossing Mexican territory are the Usumacinta, Papaloapan, Grijalva, Coatzacoalcos, Balsas, Bravo, Pánuco, Honda, Lerma-Santiago, Tecolutla, and Fuerte. Four of these rivers flow into the Gulf of Mexico and discharge a total of 2.2 million litres of water per second. The Usumacinta discharges about 900,000 litres of water per second, Grijalva 700,000, Coatzacoalcos 400,000, and the Papaloapan 200,000. The Bravo is one of longest rivers in the world, with a length of 2,800 km, as well as a maximum volume average of close to 120,000 litres per second.

5. Mexico has great climate diversity. Climates range from warm, with annual average temperatures of 26°C, to cold, with annual average temperatures of 10°C. Nevertheless, 93% of the national territory oscillates between temperatures of 10°C and 26°C; this figure includes a hot, sub-humid climate for 23% of the national territory; dry for 28%; very dry for 21%, and temperate, sub-humid for 21%.

6. Thus, because of its geographical location, form, climate, topography, and geology, Mexico presents a wide variety of ecological conditions unique in the world that give to it a great wealth of soils, mineral resources, and biodiversity. As reported by the World Bank, natural resources in Mexico are among the most bounteous in the world. With only 1.4% of the world's surface, Mexico ranks fourth in biological diversity, first in number of species of pine trees, second in reptiles, and fifth in mammals and plants. Mexico is home to an estimated 10% of all known species, many of them endemic, found nowhere else on Earth (63% of endemic flora and 30% of endemic vertebrates).

B. Population

7. Mexico is the eleventh most populated country in the world and third in the Americas (after the United States and Brazil). Conforming to the last Census of Population and Housing, in 2010, 112, 336, 538[1] people inhabited Mexico 51.2% of which are women and 48.8% are men. In consonance with official data, the rate of natural population growth – in 2010 – was 1.4%, over the official projection of 1.28%, which is above the international average of 1.2% and slightly above the average for Latin America and the Caribbean of 1.3%. Of course, the Mexican population is not uniformly distributed throughout the country.

8. The States of the north and the peninsulas (excluding Nuevo León and Yucatan) have relatively few inhabitants, especially in terms of their density. Instead, the population density is mainly located in the Federal District and its metropolitan area.

9. In terms of demographic transition, there is a homogenous situation. Whereas in the Federal District, in 2010, the fecundity rate (the number of children that a woman has throughout her life to conserve the present conditions) was less than 2, whereas in the States of Guerrero, Oaxaca, Chiapas, and Potosí San Luis, the fecundity rate was above 2.4.

10. On the other hand, during the past several years, a noticeable tendency towards urbanization has been observed. Whereas in 1900, four-fifths of the population of the country inhabited rural areas, by 2010, 78.03% of Mexicans inhabited urban zones.

11. The annual rate of growth of the rural population has not exceeded 2% per year at any time, whereas in the cities, we have been observing rates above 5%. Mexico is also the country with the greatest indigenous population on the North American Continent.

12. Throughout Mexican territory, around eighty-nine[2] indigenous languages are spoken. For the twenty-first century, 6,044,547 indigenous speakers in the country were reported, most of which also spoke Spanish. It is estimated that there are about 4 million indigenous people who speak only Spanish, although they retain other distinctive cultural elements.

13. The indigenous languages with the most number of speakers are Nahuatl, Maya, Mixteco, and Zapoteca, which comprise 52.1% of the total. Some indigenous languages are spoken by few children, such as Cucapá, Kikapú, Kiliwa, and Kumiai; this is important, considering that, by their disuse, these languages are at risk of being extinguished soon.

II. Legal and Political Structure

14. In accordance with Article 40 of the *Constitution of the United Mexican States* (hereinafter, 'the Mexican Constitution', as amended in 2012), 'It is the will of the Mexican people to constitute a representative, democratic, laic, and federal Republic

1. . *See* : http://www.inegi.org.mx/.
2. . Instituto Nacional de Estadística y Geografía, 'Conociendo México' (2012) (available at www.inegi.org.mx).

composed by States, free and sovereign in all matters concerning their internal affairs; but united in a federation established in consonance to the principles of this fundamental law.'[3]

15. In addition, Article 49 of the Mexican Constitution points out that:

> The Supreme Power of the Federation is divided for its exercise into Executive, Legislative and Judicial branches.

and adds that:

> Two or more of these powers may not be united in one single person or corporation, nor shall the legislative Power be vested in one single person, except for the case where extraordinary powers are granted to the President of the Republic as provided in Article 29. In no other case, except as provided under the second paragraph of Article 131 shall extraordinary powers be granted to legislate.

16. In accordance with constitutional provisions, in Mexico, the Executive Branch rests with a single individual, popularly elected, who holds his or her post for six years without the possibility of re-election (Articles 80, 81, and 83 of the Mexican Constitution).

17. On the other hand, the Legislative Branch is composed of the Congress of the Union, divided into two Cameras: one of Deputies, with 500 members, elected in full every three years; and the other a Chamber of Senators, with 128 representatives, four from each State and the Federal District, which is renewed every six years. (Articles 50, 51, 52, and 56 of the Mexican Constitution).

18. The exercise of the Judicial Power of the Federation is vested in the Nation's Supreme Court of Justice, composed of eleven Justices, in an Electoral Court, in Collegiate and Unitary Circuit Courts, and in District Courts (Article 94 of the Mexican Constitution).

19. In addition, Article 94 of the Constitution establishes that 'Management, supervision and discipline of the Judicial Power of the Federation, except for the Nation's Supreme Court of Justice, shall be entrusted to the Council of the Federal Judiciary.'

III. Economic Characteristics

20. Among the developing countries, Mexico is the second-most important destination for foreign direct investment and third in accumulated growth. It is second in tourism, which represents the second-greatest source of income for the country. In addition, Mexico is a world leader in silver, celestine honey, fruit, citrus, fabrics, and cement production.

21. In this context, the main source of income in Mexico is hydrocarbons production. As reported by the International Agency of Energy, Mexico is currently

3. . By constitutional reform this article was added with the word *laic.* Diario Oficial de la Federacion (DOF) 30 Nov. 2012.

the leading Latin American country in crude oil production: 3.8 million barrels per day. About one-third of State revenues come from this activity. *Petroleos Mexicanos* (PEMEX) is one of the major international producers of crude oil and the main provider to the United States.

22. Another important source of income is natural gas. Mexico is ranked fourth in reserves of this resource in Latin America but ranked third in production, with a volume of more than 36,000 million m^3. Nevertheless, given that the demand for natural gas for domestic consumption has grown noticeably in recent years, the flow of its export is modest.

23. However, currently, the second-most important source of revenue in the Country still is the workers who migrate legally and illegally to the United States of America.

IV. Social and Cultural Characteristics

24. The benefits of all the economic wealth that Mexico gets from its natural resources and the productivity of Mexicans are not equitably distributed. As reported by the World Bank, in 2004, while 10% of Mexico's population received 40% of the nation's income, 40% of the poorest population received only 12%, with some people surviving on just USD 1 per day.

25. Thus, Mexico ranks among the twelve most unequal societies in the world, not only by the disproportionate distribution of wealth, but also by the inequalities in access to education, health, water, electricity, etc., not to mention that gender inequalities remain very marked as well.

26. In recent decades, this situation has generated a greater migratory flow to the United States of America, as well as illegal trafficking of natural resources.

V. Main Environmental Problems

27. Among the main environmental problems that Mexico faces are a loss of biological diversity; soil, water, and air pollution; and inadequate management of municipal, industrial, and hazardous wastes.

28. Undoubtedly, biodiversity lost in both terrestrial ecosystems and coastal and marine ecosystems represents a serious problem. In fact, in consonance with official data, Mexico has one of the most critically threatened areas in the world; this area is located in the south of the country, in the Gulf of Tehuantepec, where two of the largest biogeographical regions of the planet – the neo-arctic and the neo-tropical – merge. Illegal trafficking of species, alteration of habitats, and commercial exploitation of flora and fauna species are the major threats to the conservation of biological diversity in Mexico.

29. On the other hand, air pollution is an almost generalized problem in the major metropolitan zones of the country, particularly in the Metropolitan Zone of the Valley of Mexico, where it has assumed critical levels. For this reason, the government is obtaining better-documented information in this area and has been trying to establish more rigorous public policies. Nevertheless, the legislative and administrative measures taken until now have far from succeeded in reducing levels of certain pollutants, such as lead, sulfur dioxide, and total suspended particles.

30. The problems of water management are very serious as well. Even though, in general, availability is greater than extraction, there are regions in the country where the extraction rate surpasses the recharge rate by far, as, for instance, in the north of the country and in the Valley of Mexico.

31. Data show that there are eighty aquifers with more than 20% of over-exploitation, which has resulted in problems of marine intrusion in the aquifers of Baja California, Baja California Sur, Sonora, and Veracruz, as well as salinity problems in Durango, Aguascalientes, and Coahuila.

32. In addition, discharges of municipal and industrial residual waters, residues of pesticides from agricultural activities, and the waste generated in the process of the extraction of minerals are the main sources of pollution of inland and marine waters.

33. In Mexico, industries annually generate about 8 million tons of hazardous waste, without considering the mining wastes that can be regarded as such, and that occur in quantities of between 300,000 and 500,000 tons per day.

34. By contrast, the existing infrastructure for the management, supervision, and control of such waste is precarious: currently, there are only two authorized disposal sites for hazardous waste in the country. Therefore, clandestine deposits of hazardous wastes are frequently discovered in municipal dumps, ravines, municipal sewers, water bodies, and, in general, in fields and other land areas of public and private ownership.

35. This situation is particularly worrisome given that almost 90% of hazardous waste is in liquid, gaseous, or semi-liquid states, or they are mixed in with waste-water discharges.

§2. Basic Principles of Environmental Law

I. Definitions and Notions

36. In accordance with Article 1 of the Ecological Equilibrium and Environmental Protection General Act (hereinafter, the Environmental Act), this law regulates the provisions of the Mexican Constitution that refer to the conservation and preservation of the ecological balance as well as environmental protection, and it pursues as a general objective the establishment of the basis for promoting sustainable development in the country. In addition, to achieve that general mission, the Environmental Act sets up the following specific objectives:

(1) to guarantee the right of all persons to live in a suitable environment for their development, health, and well-being;
(2) to define the principles of environmental policy and the instruments for its application;
(3) the preservation, restoration, and improvement of the environment;

(4) the preservation and protection of biodiversity, as well as the establishment and management of protected natural areas;
(5) the viable use, preservation, and, when appropriate, natural restoration of soil, water, and other resources, so that they make compatible the generation of economic benefits and the activities of society with the preservation of ecosystems;
(6) the prevention and control of water, air, and soil pollution;
(7) to guarantee co-responsible participation of the people, in individual or collective form, in the preservation and restoration of ecological balance and the protection of the environment;
(8) the exercise of powers that in environmental matters correspond to the Federation, the States, the Federal District, and the Municipalities, under the principle of concurrence established by Article 73, section XXIX(g) of the Mexican Constitution;
(9) the establishment of coordination mechanisms, induction, and agreement between and among authorities and the social and private sectors, as well as between people and groups, in environmental matters; and
(10) the establishment of measures of control and security to guarantee the fulfilment and application of this Law and the provisions that are derived from it, as well as the imposition of the administrative and criminal sanctions that correspond.

37. Nevertheless, to meet such objectives, the Environmental Act should clearly define the objects that it protects. In this regard, it is important to consider that the Environmental Act is intended to protect different objects, such as the environment, biodiversity, and sustainable development. In the same way, it is intended to prevent pollution, to conserve natural resources, and to preserve and restore them. Thus, it is fundamental to understand these concepts.

A. Environment

38. The environment is defined by the Environmental Act as 'the set of natural and artificial elements introduced by humans who make possible the existence and development of human beings and other living organisms that interact in a specific space and time' (Article 3, section I).

39. However, both previous legislation and the subsequent entry into force of the Environmental Act use the terms *environment, natural resources, biodiversity,* and *wildlife* to refer either to the environment as a whole or to one or many of the natural elements that comprise it (Article 1).

40. For example, the General Act of Wildlife (hereinafter, the Wildlife Act) refers to the conservation and sustainable use of wildlife and its habitat in the territory of the Mexican Republic and in the zones where it exerts its sovereignty and jurisdiction.

41. In the same way, the objective of enforcing the General Act for Sustainable Forest Development (hereinafter, Forest Act) is to 'regulate and promote conservation, protection, restoration, production, management, cultivation, and use of forest ecosystems of the country and its resources'; and the General Act for the Comprehensive Prevention and Management of Waste (hereinafter, Waste Act) is aimed at regulating only this form of pollution.

42. Despite the aforementioned issues, the Environmental Act incorporates the concept of ecological balance, which is defined as 'the relation of interdependence among the elements that compose the environment and makes possible the existence, transformation, and development of human beings and other ways of life' (Article 3, section XIV).

43. Nevertheless, incorporating the concept of the environment into the Environmental Act has not brought any consequences, neither in its regulatory structure nor in the legal institutions regulated by it, which still refer separately to the various elements of the environment, but not to the environment in and of itself.

B. Pollution

44. Fighting against pollution is, without any doubt, one of the central objectives of the Environmental Law, but its effectiveness can fail if the legislation is constructed based on a concept of pollution that is not sufficiently precise. For example, the Environmental Act defines pollution in general terms as 'the presence in the environment of one or more pollutants or any combination of them that may cause an ecological imbalance' (Article 3, section VI). However, it does not establish any criteria to determine the emission level of pollutant agents that can cause such an imbalance.

45. Moreover, normally, the administrative measures that aim to reduce and eliminate pollution are characterized by their individual application, while the environmental imbalances tend to be the result of synergies produced by several pollutant discharges combined with the action of other factors, including those not of an anthropogenic origin. Accordingly, the concept of pollution is far from being accurate.

C. Conservation

46. Conservation is an important area of environmental protection and, therefore, tends to be one of the objectives of environmental and natural resources legislation in Mexico. Mexican law has opted to use as synonyms for the term *conservation* the concepts of preservation, protection, and sustainable use of natural resources.

47. Thus, according to Environmental Act, *preservation* means 'the set of policies and measures to maintain the conditions conducive to the evolution and continuity of ecosystems and natural habitats, as well as to conserve viable populations of species in their natural environments and the components of biodiversity outside their natural habitats' (Article 3, section XXV); while *protection* includes 'the set of policies and measures to improve the environment and control its deterioration' (Article 3, section XVII). On the other hand, sustainable use is 'the use of natural resources in a form that respects the operational integrity and the capabilities of the burden of systems that are part of these resources for indefinite periods (Article 3, section III).[4]

4. . By reform of the Environmental Act published into the DOF 28 Jan. 2011, sections of Art. 3 were reorganized and the definition of 'sustainable use' was eliminated.

D. *Ecosystems and Sustainability*

48. In accordance with the Environmental Act, an *ecosystem* is 'the basic functional unit of interaction of living organisms among themselves and with the environment, in a certain space and time' (Article 3, section XIII). Moreover, this Law is the only legal instrument that refers to the concept of *sustainable development,* defining it as:

> the measurable process through criteria and indicators of environmental, economic, and social trends to improve the quality of life and the productivity of persons, which is based on appropriate measures for the preservation of the ecological balance, environmental protection, and use of natural resources, so that the satisfaction of the future generations needs is not compromised. (Article 3, section XI)

However, such a definition is very vague.

E. *Biodiversity and Ecological Integrity*

49. Biodiversity is defined by the Environmental Act as 'the variability of living organisms from any source, including, among others, terrestrial ecosystems, maritime and other aquatic ecosystems, and complex ecological systems of which such organisms are a part; comprising diversity within each species, and among species and ecosystems' (Article 3, section IV). However, biodiversity is just a part of the subject protected under the Environmental Act. As its name indicates, this Law protects the ecological balance as a whole and not the natural elements in separate ways. This means that the Environmental Act integrates in a comprehensive way the legal protection of the environment. Nevertheless, this approach is contradicted by the existence of other environmental laws that protect natural elements in separate ways.

II. Constitutional Provisions

50. Since it was approved in 1917, the Mexican Constitution included many references to the subject of natural resources protection but not to the protection of environmentas a whole.

51. However, during the period 1970–2012, the Constitution was amended six times to incorporate environmental concerns, and in 2010, 2011, and 2012, several Constitutional provisions were also modified to strength the foundations for access to environmental justice.

52. Thus, currently, the Mexican Constitution includes rules regarding the following:

(a) the protection of natural resources (Article 27);
(b) the power of the General Health Council to adopt measures to prevent and combat environmental pollution (Article 73, section XVI, paragraph 4);

(c) the relationship between environment and social and economic development (Article 25);
(d) the preservation and restoration of the ecological balance and environmental protection (Articles 27 and 73, section XXIX(g));
(e) the distribution of powers between the States and the Federation in environmental matters (Article 73, section XXIX(g));
(f) the right to a healthy environment (Article 4); this right is considerate as human right by the amendment of 2011);[5]
(g) the right to access to water (Article 4)
(h) the principle of liability for environmental damage (Article 4 second paragraph as amended 2012);[6]
(i) the legal standing to file collective actions in environmental matters (Article 17, third paragraph, as amended in 2010);[7] and
(j) the recognition of collective legal interest to file injunction actions to combat unconstitutional resolutions issued by environmental authorities (Article 107, section I as amended in 2011).[8]

The following sections will explain the process of evolution of constitutional basis of Mexican environmental law.

A. Article 27 of the Mexican Constitution of 1917 and Natural Resources Protection

53. For many years, Article 27 of the Mexican Constitution provided enough basis for legislation on natural resources protection. First, the first paragraph of Article 27 as it was passed in 1917 recognized that the original property of the lands and waters of the Mexican territory was vested in the Nation and it had the power of transferring their domain to private persons to create private property on land and waters. Second, conforming paragraph two of Article 27, the State can use its power of eminent domain to compel a private property owner to relinquish ownership and dominion of any property to the state, but it only may be taken for reasons of public use and subject to payment compensation.

54. Third, paragraph 3 of Article 27 empowered the nation to impose on private property such restrictions as the public interest may demand, as well as to regulate, for social benefit, the use and exploitation of those natural resources, which are susceptible of appropriation.

55. Finally, paragraphs 4 and 5 of Article 27 provided basis for the rectory of the state on the use, exploitation, and conservation of certain natural resources considered as strategic. In consonance with them, waters and natural resources of the subsoil are considered as exclusive property of the Nation and, therefore, can only be exploited by individuals through the granting of concessions and contracts in the case of

5. . DOF, 10 Jun. 2011.
6. . DOF, 08 Feb. 2012.
7. . DOF, 29 Jul. 2010.
8. . DOF, 06 Jun. 2011.

hydrocarbons, but the domain of the Nation on the mentioned resources is inalienable and imprescriptible.

Based on such constitutional provisions the Federal Congress passed the Federal Law to Prevent and Combat Pollution of 1972 and the Federal Environmental Protection Act of 1981.

B. Article 73, Section XVI of the Mexican Constitution of 1917 and the Faculties of the General Council of Health to Adopt Measures to Prevent and to Deal with Environmental Pollution

56. The ideas of preventing and combating environmental pollution, as an important part of environmental law, were expressly included into the Constitutional text with the Reform of 1971, which added a fourth paragraph to section XVI of Article 73 of the Constitution.[9] That Reform empowered the General Health Council to adopt measures aimed at preventing and to combating environmental pollution. In addition, the constitutional reform empowered the Federal Congress to review the measures made by the Council by saying:

> 4° The measures that the Council has put into effect in the campaign against alcoholism and the sale of substances that poison individuals or degenerate the human species, as well as those measures adopted to prevent and fight against environmental pollution, shall thereafter be examined by the Congress of the Union in the cases under its jurisdiction.

C. Article 25 of the Mexican Constitution of 1917 and the Relationship Between Environment and Social and Economic Development (Article 25)

57. Article 25 of the Mexican Constitution has been also modified twice regarding the ideas of sustainability and social and economic development, as explained below.

58. In 1983, Article 25 of the Mexican Constitution was amended to include a reference to the relationship between the environment and economic development as follows:

> Under criteria of social equity and productivity, enterprises of the social and private sectors of the economy will be supported and encouraged, holding them to the modalities issued by the public interest and to the use, in general benefit, of productive resources, taking care of their conservation and the environment.

59. For some authors, that reform established the principles that give substance to the model of sustainable development in Mexico. However, the constitutional basis of sustainable development in Mexico was not introduced with the 1983´s amendment to Article 25, but with two other constitutional amendments. First, the reform of 1987 to Article 27 that not only establishes the exclusive property of the Nation over certain

9. . DOF, 06 Jul. 1971.

natural resources, but also empowers it to impose modalities on private property in cases where the elements of the environment form part of this patrimonial regime or to regulate their use when considered as *res nullius*.

60. Second, the reform of 1999 to Article 25, that expressly included the concept of sustainability into the constitutional text. New article wording is as follows:

> The State has the responsibility for the direction of national development; to ensure that this is integrated and sustainable; to strengthen the sovereignty of the nation and its democratic system, and that through the promotion of economic growth and employment and a fairer distribution of income and wealth, there will occur the full exercise of freedom and dignity of individuals, groups, and social classes, whose security protects this Constitution.

D. The Amendment of 1987 to Articles 25 and 73, Section XXIX- G

61. In 1987, an important reform to Articles 27 and 73 of the Constitution was passed.[10] The amendment to Article 27 ruled that the exercise of the powers of the Nation to impose on private property those modalities dictated by the public interest or to regulate the use of natural elements susceptible of appropriation, should have as an objective – among others – the preservation and restoration of the ecological balance.

62. Thus, the mentioned provision was worded as follows:

> The Nation will have at any time the right to impose on private property those modalities dictated by the public interest, as well as to regulate, for social benefit, the development of the natural elements susceptible to appropriation, to make possible an equitable distribution of public wealth, taking care for their conservation, to achieve a balanced development of the country and to improve the life of the rural and urban population. Thus, the Nation will take the necessary steps for managing human settlements and establishing adequate provisions, uses, reservations, and destinations of land, water, and forests to execute public works and plan and regulate the foundation, conservation, improvement, and growth of the population centres; **to preserve and restore the ecological balance** …

63. With this reform, for the first time, the possibility of expanding the range of legal mechanisms to protect the environment, and not only natural resources as foreseen by the pristine text of Article 27 of the Constitution, was opened.

E. The Distribution of Powers Between the States and the Federation in Environmental Matters (Article 73, Section XXIX(g))

64. The aforementioned constitutional reform passed in 1987 also introduced the system of concurrent competences on the matters of environmental protection and restoration of ecological balance, under the premise that in environmental issues it is

10. DOF, 10 Aug. 1987.

not convenient to centralize functions, but it requires the participation of all levels of authority.

65. This amendment allowed the thirty-two entities comprising the Federal pact – including Mexico′s City – to issue their own local environmental laws and allowed the municipalities to dictate ordinances and regulations on environmental matters. Thus, based on this amendment, the protection of the environment had to be regarded as a case in which the three levels of government are competent to legislate.

66. The Federal Congress for the first time interpreted the Constitutional reform of 1987 when it passed the General Law on Ecological Equilibrium and Environmental Protection.[11] Article 1, section VII established as one of its objectives to set up the bases for the concurrence of the federal government, local governments, and the municipalities in this matter, and Chapter II of the First Title established the rules that govern concurrent jurisdictions system.

67. The Constitutional reform of 1987 is particularly relevant, as it, for the first time, gave the Constitution a clear basis for the enactment of specific laws in the field of environmental protection, and not just regarding natural resources protection.

68. In 2001, the Supreme Court of the Justice of the Nation, in ruling on a constitutional controversy filed by the federal government against the Government of Mexico City in relation to the Education Law of the Federal District, resolved, that section XXIX-G of Article 73 of the Constitution must be interpreted as meaning that the Congress of the Union is empowered to issue general environmental laws that distribute powers between the Federation, the States, the Federal District, and the municipalities, and on the other hand established the Federal system regulating the performance of the central powers in the matter in question. Since this is a decision on a constitutional controversy, it constitutes binding jurisprudence. The thesis is as follows:

> CONCURRING FACULTIES IN THE MEXICAN LEGAL SYSTEM. GENERAL CHARACTERISTICS. Although article 124 of the Political Constitution of the United States of Mexico establishes that: 'Powers not expressly granted by this Constitution to federal officials are understood to be reserved to States.' The Reforming organ of the Constitution determined, in various precepts, the possibility that the Congress of the Union would establish a division of powers, called 'concurrent faculties', between the Federation, the federal entities and the municipalities, and even the Federal District, in some areas, such as education (Article 3, section VIII and 73, section XXV), health (articles 4, paragraph 3 and 73, section XVI), human settlements (articles 27, third paragraph And Article 73, section XXIX-C), public security (article 73, section XXIII), environmental protection (article 73, section XXIX-G), civil protection (article 73, section XXIX-I) and sports Article 73, section XXIX-J). That is, in the Mexican legal system the concurrent faculties imply that the federal entities, including the Federal District, the Municipalities and the Federation, can act on the same matter, but it will be the Congress of the Union that determines the form and the terms of participation of the entities through a general law.

11. This Law was passed by the Federal Congress in 1987 but it was published into the DOF on 28 Jan. 1988.

Constitutional controversy 29/2000. Federal Executive Power. November 15, 2001. Eleven votes. Speaker: Sergio Salvador Aguirre Anguiano. Secretary: Pedro Alberto Nava Malagón.

The Plenum Tribunal, at its private meeting held in December 6, approved, with number 142/2001, the jurisprudential thesis above. Mexico, Federal District, on December 6, two thousand and one.

69. In fact, as already mentioned, the enactment of the General Law on Ecological Equilibrium and Environmental Protection has followed by the entry into force of other general laws approved based on the same constitutional provision already mentioned, which also distribute powers between states and the Federation.

F. *Article 4 of the Mexican Constitution of 1917 and the Right to a Healthy Environment*

70. The right to a healthy environment as a fundamental right set forth in the Mexican Constitution was incorporated in the amendment of 1999 to Article 4. That amendment added a fourth paragraph to the mentioned article, which states: 'Every person has the right to a suitable environment for his or her development and welfare.' By Constitutional reform passed in 2011, this fourth paragraph was moved to fifth paragraph.[12]

71. By Constitutional reform of June 2011, the right to a healthy environment, as well as other fundamental rights were considered human rights instead of individual warranties.

G. *Article 4 of the Mexican Constitution of 1917 and the Right of Access to Water*

72. The background to the incorporation of the right of access to water and sanitation can be found in various documents of an international nature, including:

- *Observation number* 15 of the Committee on Economic, Social, and Cultural Rights 2002, and
- Resolution 64/292, the United Nations General Assembly of 28 July 2010.

Council's *observation number 15*, Article I.1, stated that 'The human right to water is indispensable for a dignified human life.' The same document defines the right to water as the right of everyone to have sufficient, healthy, acceptable, physically accessible, and affordable water for their personal and domestic use.

73. The United Nations Resolution recognizes that '*the* right to safe drinking water and sanitation is an essential human right to the full enjoyment of life and all human rights' and 'urges States and international organizations to provide financial resources and to enhance capacity and technology, transfer through international

12. DOF, 13 Oct. 2011.

assistance and cooperation, particularly to developing countries, in order to intensify efforts to the entire population an economic access to drinking water and sanitation'.

74. With this background, a constitutional reform of 2012 adds to Article 4 of the Mexican Constitution a sixth paragraph that provides:

> Everyone has the right to adequate, safe, acceptable and affordable access, disposal and sanitation of water for personal and domestic consumption. The State will guarantee this right and the law will define the basis, supports and modalities for the access and equitable and sustainable use of water resources, establishing the participation of the Federation, the federal entities and the municipalities, as well as the participation of citizenship for the attainment of these purposes.

75. The new precept adopted the same formula that in this moment was used when recognizing the right to a healthy environment, it gives the State the responsibility to guarantee this right and it transfers to the secondary legislation the obligation to define its content and scope. The constitutional precept indicates that this right must guarantee a sufficient, healthy, acceptable, and affordable access but it does not clarify what is meant by each one of these concepts. Secondary legislation is expected to address the issue.

76. In fact, the Decree that promulgated the mentioned reform contains a Third Transitory article that obliges the Congress of the Union to issue a General Law of Waters a term of 360 days. Although the new law has not yet been approved, the General Law initiative that has been submitted to the consideration of the Congress of the Union contains a Second Title called 'Human Right to Water' that is integrated by Articles 40–53. Article 46 of the initiative states that 'norms relating to the human right to water shall be interpreted in accordance with the Political Constitution of the United Mexican States and international treaties of the subject, always favouring persons the widest protection'.

H. Article 4 of the Mexican Constitution of 1917 and the Principle of Liability for Environmental Damage

77. In 2012, fifth paragraph of Article 4 of the Constitution was added with a second part which states: 'Those generated environmental damage are liable in the terms set forth by the law.' A transitory provision of this last amended obliged the Federal Congress to pass a law regulating liability for environmental damages in a term of six months from the day the constitutional amendment came into force. Based on this constitutional reform, in 2013 the Federal Congress passed the Federal Environmental Liability Act.[13]

13. DOF, 07 Jun. 2013.

I. Article 17 of the Mexican Constitution of 1917 and the Legal Standing to File Collective Actions in Environmental Matters

78. As mentioned before, during the twenty-first century, several constitutional reforms have been passed with the aim of making possible access to environmental justice. The first constitutional reform was passed in July 2010.[14]

79. The new provision obliged the Federal Congress to pass a law regulating collective actions, including judicial procedures and a mechanism for the restoration of environmental damage. In consonance with this Constitutional reform, jurisdiction to decide on these matters is vested in federal judges. Thus, in 2012 the Federal Code of Civil Procedure was added with a fifth Book that regulates collective actions.[15]

J. Article 107 of the Mexican Constitution of 1917 and the Recognition of Collective Legal Interest to File Injunction Actions to Combat Unconstitutional Resolutions Issue by Environmental Authorities

80. A second constitutional reform, which modified Articles 94, 103, 104, and 107 of the Federal Constitution, was passed in 2011.[16] These articles regulate one of the most important instruments for human rights protection in Mexico: the Amparo Trial (injunction). However, these provisions were crafted to protect only individual interest. The reform to Article 107 means that for the first time an *amparo* action may be filed not only to protect individual and direct interests, as the original text of the Constitution provided, but also in defence of the indirect and collective legal interests, such as the collective interest in protecting the environment. Article 107 as amended reads as follows:

> Article 107. All dispute considered under article 103 shall be subject of the proceeding and formalities established by the law, in accordance with the following bases:
>
> "The Amparo trial must always be initiated at instance of injury party, having this character those who argument to have a right or individual or collective legitimate interest, under the condition that the act claimed violets a right recognized by this Constitution and with that it its juridical interest directly or because its especial legal situation"

Based in this constitutional reform, in 2013 the Federal Congress passed a new Law ruling the Amparo Trial.[17]

14. DOF, 29 Jul. 2010.
15. DOF, 09 Apr. 2012.
16. DOF, 06 Jun. 2011.
17. DOF, 02 Apr. 2013.

K. The New General Laws

81. Given that section XXIX(g) of Article 73 of the Mexican Constitution allows the enactment of several general laws, so far during the twenty-first century, the Federal Congress has enacted: (a) the General Act of Wildlife of 2000 (Wildlife Act as amended in 2010);[18] (b) the General Act for Sustainable Forest Development of 2003[19] (Forest Act as amended in 2005 and 2008); (c) the General Act for Prevention and Integral Management of Waste of 2003[20] (Waste Act as amended in 2006 and 2007); (d) the General Act of Sustainable Fisheries and Aquaculture of 2007[21] (amended in 2012); (e) the General Act of climate change of 2012;[22] (f) the Federal Environmental Liability Act of 2013,[23] the General Act of Human Settlements, Territorial Ordinance and Urban Development of 2016[24]; while the National Waters Act (Water Act of 1992) was substantially modified in 2004.

§4. Role of Government Institutions in the Shaping and Administration of Environmental Law and Policy

82. In 1972, the Undersecretary for the Improvement of the Environment was established within the structure of the Ministry of Public Health with the objective of enforcing the Federal Law to Prevent and Control Environmental Pollution of 1971.

83. Nevertheless, given that Environmental Act of 1972 did not regulate all aspects related to environmental protection but only those regarding environmental pollution, and given that protection of natural elements such as terrestrial and aquatic flora and fauna were the subjects of other legal instruments whose application was not entrusted to the Federal governmental level, other administrative agencies participated in environmental management as well.

84. The Ministry of Hydraulic Resources was responsible for the matters of prevention and control of water pollution, the Ministry of Agriculture was responsible for the matters of prevention and control of soil pollution, and the Ministry of Industry and Trade was responsible for the matters of prevention and control of industrial and commercial pollutant activities.

85. In 1982, the Ministry of Urban Development and Ecology was created to enforce both urban and environmental laws. Thus, the Ministry of Urban Development and Ecology concentrated on the Authority that had previously rested with the Ministries of the Environments of Agriculture and Hydraulic Resources, Public Health, and Fishing.

86. The Ministry of the Urban Development and Ecology was eliminated in 1992, when the Ministry of Social Development was created and it was vested with

18. . DOF, 03 Jul. 2010.
19. . DOF, 25 Feb. 2003.
20. . DOF, 08 Oct. 2003.
21. . DOF, 24 Jul. 2007.
22. . DOF, 06 Jun. 2012.
23. . DOF, 07 Jun. 2013.
24. . DOF, 29 Nov. 2016.

the Authority to enforce the law in some areas of environmental protection, whereas other areas were reassigned to the Ministries of Agriculture and of Hydraulic Resources and to the Ministry of Fishing and the Ministry Maritime Affairs.

87. The new Ministry was vested with few of the responsibilities that had previously corresponded to the Ministry of Urban Development and Ecology. Within the new Ministry, two administrative bodies were created. The National Institute of Ecology was constituted as the body in charge of regulating different aspects that fall under the aegis of environmental matters. On the other hand, the Federal Attorney General's Office for Environmental Protection oversaw exercising authority in the matters of inspection and monitoring compliance with environmental legislation within the sphere of responsibility of the Ministry of Social Development.

88. Nevertheless, other offices of the Federal government, such as the Ministries of Agriculture and Hydraulic Resources, the Ministry of Fishing, and the Ministry of Maritime Affairs were entrusted with the enforcement of specific environmental laws.

89. In 1994, the Ministry of the Environment, Natural Resources, and Fishing was created. As had happened in the case of the Ministry of Urban Development and Ecology, all the functions in the field of compliance with and enforcement of environmental legislation were assigned to the new Ministry.

90. The Federal Attorney General's Office for Environmental Protection, the National Institute of Ecology, and other agencies, such as the National Waters Commission (NWC), and the National Institute of Fishing, which previously had been separate entities, were grouped into the new Ministry of the Environment.

91. Finally, in the year 2000, enforcement of fishing law was transferred to the Ministry of Agriculture, and the Ministry of the Environment, Natural Resources, and Fishing was transformed into the Ministry of the Environment and Natural Resources.

I. The Governmental Institutions and Their Competencies

92. In Mexico, environmental management is distributed among Federal, local, and municipal Authorities in accordance with provisions of the Environmental Act, the Wildlife Act, the Forest Act, the Waste Act, the Climate Change Act, and the General Act of Human Settlements, Territorial Ordinance, and Urban Development.

93. Conforming to Article 32*bis* of the Organic Law of the Federal Public Administration, it falls to the Ministry of the Environment and Natural Resources (Ministry of the Environment) to formulate and conduct national policy in the matters of natural resources, ecology, environmental cleaning, water, and environmental regulation of urban development, and fishing activities.

94. Nevertheless, in concordance with the mentioned Law, the Ministry of the Environment has limited jurisdiction. It can take care of matters of natural resources only when they do not correspond to another governmental agency, as in the case of waters and marine zones, which are under the jurisdiction of the Ministry of Marine Affairs, or in the case of urban lands, whose regulation is governed by the Ministry of Agrarian, Territorial, and Urban Development.

95. On the other hand, in relation to the formulation and conduction of policy in the matters of ecology, environmental cleaning, water, environmental regulation of urban development and fishing activities, the jurisdiction of the Ministry of the Environment is not absolute, but other agencies take part as well, as in the case of environmental pollution when it becomes a matter of public health and moves to the scope of competence of the Ministry of Health; or in the promotion of forest plantations, in which case the Ministry of the Environment must allow the participation of the Ministry of Agriculture, Livestock, Rural Development, Fisheries, and Feeding (Ministry of Agriculture). The situation is different regarding the formulation and conduction of policy in the matters of climatic change and the protection of the ozone layer, since, in both cases, authority is designated exclusively to the Ministry of the Environment.

96. In addition to its mentioned authority, the Ministry of the Environment is entrusted with regulatory Authority, such as the elaboration and promulgation of environmental standards that establish maximum limits of emission of pollutant agents, the authorization of the evaluation of environmental impact, or the authorization of management of natural resources. The Ministry of the Environment also has the power to enforce environmental legislation through its semi-autonomous agencies Environmental Prosecutor, National Waters Commission, and the Environmental Agency for Hydrocarbons Sector.

97. On the other hand, State and municipal governments have created institutions in charge of environmental management as well. In some of the States that are part of the Mexican Federation, as in the States of Guanajuato and Guerrero, the Attorney General's Offices enforce local environmental laws; whereas in other States, such task has been entrusted to the Ministries of the Environment.

II. The Actual Role of the Governmental Institutions

98. Currently, the Ministry of the Environment and Natural Resources leads environmental management in Mexico at the federal level, whereas in some cases, local governments have created specialized institutions or have entrusted previously existing institutions to enforce the local legislation.

99. The Ministry of the Environment exerts its authority through three Undersecretary's offices and several semi-autonomous agencies. The Undersecretary's offices are:

(a) The Undersecretary of Planning and Environmental Policy,
(b) The Undersecretary of Promotion and Environmental Standardization, and
(c) The Undersecretary of Management for Environmental Protection.

100. The semi-autonomous agencies are:

(a) The National Waters Commission (NWC),
(b) The National Institute of Ecology,
(c) The Federal Attorney General's Office for Environmental Protection (Environmental Prosecutor),
(d) The National Commission of Protected Natural Areas (NCPNA), and

(e) The National Agency for Industrial Safety and Environmental Protection of the Hydrocarbons Sector (Environmental Agency for Energy Sector).

101. The Environmental Prosecutor, the NWC, and the Environmental Agency for Hydrocarbons Sector are vested with authoritative functions. In general terms, the Environmental Prosecutor oversees the enforcement of environmental legislation, excepting the National Waters Law, whose enforcement is entrusted to the NWC and excepting the enforcement of environmental legislation in the case of hydrocarbons activities that is vested in the Environmental Agency for Hydrocarbons Sector.

102. In the same way, given the concurrent jurisdictions system established by Mexican Constitution, all local governments have already established their own environmental law enforcement authorities.

§5. Sources of Environmental Law

I. International Sources

103. The fundamental source of environmental law in Mexico is international treaties. Mexico has subscribed to nearly seventy international treaties that include subjects related to the conservation and protection of the environment, among them are the following:

- The Convention on Wetlands of International Importance, especially as Waterfowl Habitats, 1971.
- The Convention Regarding the Protection of the Cultural and Natural Patrimony of Humanity, 1972.
- The Convention on the Prevention of Marine Pollution by Dumping of Wastes and Other Matter, 1972.
- The Convention on International Trade in Endangered Species of Wild Flora and Fauna (CITES), Washington, DC, 1973.
- The International Convention for the Prevention of Pollution from Ships, London, 1973, as modified by the Protocol of 1978 relating thereto (MARPOL).
- The Convention of the United Nations on the Right of the Sea, 1982.
- The Basel Convention on the Control of Transboundary Movements of Hazardous Wastes and their Disposal, 1989.
- The Vienna Convention for the Protection of the Ozone Layer, 1985.
- The Convention on Biological Diversity, 1992.
- The United Nations Framework Convention on Climate Change, 1992.
- The United Nations Convention to Combat Desertification, 1994.

104. Similarly, Mexico has signed many of international declarations in the field of environmental protection, such as the Declaration of the United Nations Conference on the Human Environment (1972), the Rio Declaration on Environment and Development (1992); the Johannesburg Declaration on Sustainable Development (2002); and the Río+20 Declaration: The future we want of 2012.

105. The Mexican Constitution recognizes the supremacy of international treaties in Article 133, which holds that:

> This Constitution, the laws of the Congress of the Union which shall be enacted in pursuance thereof and all treaties in accordance therewith, celebrated or which shall be celebrated by the President of the Republic with the approval of the Senate, shall be a supreme law of the Union. The judges of the Federal District and of the States shall be bound thereby, notwithstanding any provision to the contrary in the local constitutions or local laws.

106. Although for many years, the Supreme Court of Justice of the Nation held that international treaties were hierarchically at the same level of the federal laws, in 1999 and 2007, it issued a new decision which states that international treaties are held hierarchically above federal laws and in a second plan regarding the Federal Constitution. Finally, in 2013, the Supreme Court of Justice ruled that International Treatises regarding human rights are hierarchically at the same level than the Constitution.

II. National Sources

A. *The Constitution and National Laws*

107. At the national level, the first source of environmental law is the Constitution, particularly Articles 4o, 25, 27 and 73, section XXIX(g), whose content has been analysed above. More specifically, general environmental laws passed by the Federal Congress, on such Constitutional basis, are the foundation for local laws in the areas of environmental protection, waters, waste and forests, as well as for municipal regulations in these areas.

B. *Doctrine*

108. Whereas in many countries, law treatises, particularly those written from the perspective of public law, have contributed not only to the best interpretation of environmental legal regimes, but also, in some cases, to its development, in Mexico, the role of scholars in the field of environmental law is still precarious.

109. By 1988, when the Environmental Act went into force, just one book on environmental law had been written in Mexico, and although by 2011 a dozen texts on the subject had been published, most them are not well documented or are only partially developed.

110. However, one must recognize the influence of the pioneering work of Ramon Ojeda Mestre, founder of the Mexican Academy of Environmental Law more than twenty-five years ago, in teaching and research on environmental law, as well as the work of Carmen Carmona, whose bachelor's degree thesis in the 1980s focused on that subject.

111. On the same plane, the work written by Raul Brañes in 1988 and re-edited in 1994 and in 2000 by the Fund of Economic Culture, entitled Manual of Mexican Environmental Rights, is – although a descriptive work – a systematic handbook that refers to all areas of Mexican environmental law.

112. At the present time, one of the most proactive institutions in promoting the study of Mexican environmental law is the Metropolitan Autonomous University, Campus Azcapotzalco, whose Department of Law has published five books on the subject and since 1993 has offered four postgraduate courses in environmental law.

113. Currently, that institution has opened a Master Degree Environmental law Programme.

114. At the same time, the *Mexican Journal of Environmental Legislation*, founded in 1999, is one of the main sources of the generation of new and serious knowledge in the legal discipline of environmental law.

C. *Jurisprudence (Judicial Decisions)*

115. In Mexico, Judiciary power has played different roles in the field of environmental protection. It has acted:

(a) as controller of administrative enforcement,
(b) as protector of the right to a healthy environment, and
(c) as interpreter of the environmental rules established by the Constitution.

1.TheJudiciary as Controller of Administrative Enforcement

116. The first role of the courts in the field of environmental protection was as reviser of the administrative Authorities' enforcement activities. The Supreme Court of Justice has adopted nearly a hundred of Judicial rulings revising acts of the administrative Authorities during the administrative procedure of environmental law enforcement.

2. The Judiciary and the Right to a Healthy Environment

117. By the 1990s, the role of the Judiciary started to focus more on issues related to the rights to information and public participation in the decision-making process as a way of protecting the right to a healthy environment.

118. In 1996, a non-governmental organization called 'The hundred international' – *Grupo de los cien internacional* – filed an injunction action (amparo) to combat an Administrative Resolution issued by the General Director of Legal Affairs of the Ministry of the Environment. This Resolution had rejected the petition formulated by 'The hundred international' requesting the Ministry of the Environment to revise a Decision through which that Ministry exempted from environmental impact authorization several industrial activities. The petitioners believed that the Ministerial Decision was contrary to the right to a healthy environment recognized by the General Law of Ecological Equilibrium and Environmental Protection (LGEEPA) and by many of international agreements adopted by the Mexican government.

119. The Fifth District Court of Mexico City that decided the case held that the petitioners had no legal standing to file the injunction action because the Ministerial Decision did not directly affect them.

120. However, the Court of Appeals (Primer Tribunal Colegiado en Materia Administrativa) that revised the Judicial ruling made by the District Court reversed the first Judicial ruling based on the argument that the recognition of the right to information by Article 33 of LGEEPA meant that the petitioners had legal standing to participate in protecting the environment, and consequently it asserted that all people have legal standing to intervene and participate in enforcing environmental laws and regulations.

121. In a similar case filed in 1997 by the Union of environmentalist groups, the Council for the Defence of the Pacific Coast, Green Peace Mexico, and the Mexican Centre of Environmental Law against the same Ministerial Decision analysed in the previously mentioned case, a District Court decided that the petitioners had no legal standing to file the injunction action. Different from what happened in the case of 1996, the new Judicial ruling was confirmed by the Court of Appeals.

122. In another injunction case filed in 1997 by the Foundation to Environmental Education, the Supreme Court of Justice held that the community had the legal standing to file an injunction action because of the collective character of environmental rights.

123. Currently, legal stand to combat administrative decisions issued by environmental authorities is widely recognized by Constitution as well as by the environmental Act.[25]

3. The Judiciary as Interpreter of the Environmental Rules Recognized by the Constitution

124. The role of Judiciary as interpreter of environmental rules recognized by the Constitution can be seen in the Case *Convimar v. Federal Government*. In 1994, the company Convimar, S.A. de C.V filed an injunction action against the environmental standard "Norma Oficial Mexicana de Emergencia (NOM-EM-136-ECOL-2002, protección ambiental-especificaciones para la conservación de mamíferos marinos en cautiverio)", arguing that paragraph 5.8.7 and 5.8.7.1 prohibited temporal or itinerant exhibition of cetaceans. The Fourth Administrative Appeals Court rejected the petition, considering that, in accordance with Articles 4o, paragraph 4, Article 25, paragraph 6, and Article 73, paragraph XXIX(g) of the Federal Constitution, the protection of a healthy environment, natural resources, and environmental restoration are fundamental principles protected by the Constitution, so that even when it does not establish the way to protect such principles, by definition its content is a matter of a systematic and comprehensive interpretation of the different laws and statutes that address this objective.

125. In the same vein, in 2000, the Supreme Court of Justice adopted an important decision interpreting Article 73, paragraph XXIX(g) of the Federal Constitution that established a rule stating that the power to enact laws regarding environmental protection is shared by the Federal and local governments. The Supreme Court decided –

25. . Legitimate interest is recognized by the Arts 17 and 107 of Federal Constitution, and by Art. 180 of the Environmental Law.

corresponding to the Federal Congress' enacting of general laws – to distribute jurisdiction among the three levels of government to legislate environmental matters.

Part I. Pollution Control

Chapter 1. General Law

§1. The Environmental Impact Assessment

126. The Environmental Impact Assessment (EIA) is an administrative procedure aimed at preventing environmental degradation and protecting natural resources. Hence, this section will begin with an analysis of the legal frame that governs this institution.

I. Concept

127. Article 28 of the Environmental Act defines the EIA as 'the procedure through which the Ministry of the Environment establishes the conditions that will govern the conduction of works or activities that may causes ecological imbalance or may surpass the limits and conditions set up by the applicable provisions to protect the environment and to preserve and to restore the ecosystems, to avoid or to reduce to the minimum their negative effects on the environment'.

128. Consequently, it is possible to assert that the EIA is an instrument of environmental policy that is of a preventive nature and assumes the form of a *sui generis* administrative procedure.

129. The EIA is of a preventive nature, because, in line with the first paragraph of Article 28 of the Environmental Act, only those activities that would cause an ecological imbalance or would surpass the limits and conditions established by the applicable legal provisions aimed at protecting the environment and at preserving and restoring ecosystems should be evaluated.

130. On the other hand, the evaluation of the environmental impact is a sui generis procedure, because first, different from what happens in other administrative procedures, during the process of evaluation, public participation of communities that could result affected by the final resolution is allowed; and second, the administrative decisions issued by the Ministry of the Environment have a regulatory character.

II. Legal Framework

131. At the Federal level, the EIA procedure is governed by:

(a) The Environmental Act,
(b) The Regulations under the Environmental Act regarding to EIA of 2000, and
(c) The Federal Act of Administrative Procedure (FAAP).

However, because of the concurrent jurisdictions system in environmental matters established by the Mexican Constitution, local environmental laws regulate the procedure of EIA as well.

132. Conforming to Articles 5, section X and 28 of the Environmental Act, the Federal environmental authorities evaluate the environmental impact of works or activities listed in Article 28, while in agreement with section XVI of Article 7, as well as to Article 32*bis* 2 of the Environmental Act, local governments are empowered to evaluate the environmental impact that could be caused by works or activities not included in those listed in Article 28.

III. Works and Activities Requiring Environmental Impact Authorization Granted by the Ministry of the Environment.

133. As mentioned above, Article 28 of the Environmental Act lists in twelve sections the works and activities subject to the previous evaluation of their environmental impact. The list includes the following works and activities:[26]

I. Hydraulic facilities, general ways of communication, pipelines, gas lines, carbon ducts, and poly ducts;

II. The petroleum, petro chemistry, chemistry, steel, wastebasket, sugar bowl, cement-production industries and electricity generation;

III. Exploration, exploitation, and benefit of minerals and substances reserved to the Federation in the terms of the Mining Laws and Regulations of Article 27 of the Mexican Constitution in nuclear matters;

IV. Treatment facilities, disposition, or elimination of hazardous wastes, as well as radioactive residuals;

V. Forest uses in tropical forests and species of difficult regeneration;

26. Original Text of Art. 28 had thirteen sections but s. VI was repealed.

VI. (repealed);

VII. Changes of uses of the Land of forest areas, as well as in forests and arid areas;

VIII. Industrial parks where the occurrence of highly risky activities is foreseen;

IX. Urban developments that affect the coastal ecosystems;

X. Works and activities in wetlands, swamps, lagoons, rivers, lakes, and connected tidelands as well as on their coasts or Federal areas;

XI. Works and activities in natural Federally protected areas;

XII. Fishing or agricultural activities that could endanger the preservation of species or lives, or cause damage to ecosystems, and

XIII. Works or activities that relate to matters of Federal competition that could cause serious and irreparable ecological imbalances, damage to public health or ecosystems, or that surpass the limits and conditions set forth in the legal provisions relative to preservation of the ecological balance and protection of the environment.

134. This list is general in nature; there are several situations that may modify its content.

135. First, the Environmental Act points out that the Regulations in this field shall specify their scope. In this sense, the final part of Article 28 paragraph 1 of the Environmental Act mandates that the Regulations shall determine in detail the works and activities that must be evaluated, as follows:

> In the cases determined by the Regulations that will be issued, those who seek to carry out some…works or activities will require the previous authorization of environmental impact granted by the Secretary.

136. Second, in its penultimate paragraph, Article 28 the Environmental Act establishes that the Regulations for the EIA shall define the works or activities that, despite being included in the list, are exempted from evaluation in the following terms:

> The Regulation under the present Law shall determine the works or activities that, because of their location, dimensions, characteristics, or scope, do not

produce significant environmental impacts, do not cause or may not cause ecological imbalances, nor surpass the limits and conditions established by legal provisions regarding the preservation of ecological balance and environmental protection, should not be submitted to the procedure of environmental impact assessment.

137. Third, section XIII of Article 28 of the Environmental Act allows the Ministry of the Environment to demand the evaluation of environmental impact of certain works or activities not included into the list. This section points out that the Ministry of Environment and Natural Resources shall require environmental impact authorization in cases of 'works or activities that relate to matters under Federal jurisdiction that could cause serious and irreparable ecological imbalances, damage to public health or ecosystems, or surpass the limits and conditions established by the legal provisions regarding the preservation of ecological balance and environmental protection'.

138. Finally, the Environmental Act also establishes a series of cases in which works or activities included in sections I to XII of Article 28 do not require evaluation of the environmental impact, and therefore, those interested in its realization shall instead simply present a preventive report to the environmental authority to evaluate their environmental impact.

139. In this sense, Article 31 of the Environmental Act points out that the works and activities referred to in sections I to XII of Article 28 require the preparation of a preventive report instead of an EIA in the following cases:

(1) When there are Official Mexican Norms (OMNs) or other provisions that regulate emissions, discharges, uses of natural resources, and, in general, all environmental impacts that could be produced by such works or activities.
(2) When the works or activities are included in a partial plan of urban development or in an ecological zoning programme that has been previously evaluated by the Secretary.
(3) When Facilities are in industrial parks authorized in the terms of the present section.

140. In all other cases, the EIA must be submitted in the 'particular modality'. The fundamental difference between 'particular' and 'regional' modalities lies in the level of detail with which the demonstration of the environmental impact must be drawn up.

IV. The Environmental Impact Statement and Its Content

141. In accordance with Article 30 of the Environmental Act, those interested in obtaining environmental impact authorization must submit to the Ministry of the Environment an environmental impact statement, which should contain, at least:

(a) a description of the possible effects on the ecosystems that could be affected by the work or activity in question, including the entirety of the elements that make up these ecosystems;
(b) the actions to prevent, mitigate or to avoid and reduce to the minimum the negative effects on the environment; and
(c) a study of risk in the case of activities considered highly risky conforming to the Environmental Act.

142. However, the Regulations for the EIA points out that the environmental impact statement may have either a 'particular' or a 'regional' character (Article 10). In accordance with Article 11, the environmental impact statement must be elaborated upon from a regional perspective only in the cases of:

(a) Industrial and aquaculture parks, aquaculture farms bigger than 500 hectares, roads and railways, projects of nuclear energy generation, dams and, in general, projects that alter the watersheds.
(b) A set of works or activities that are included in a plan or partial programme of urban development or environmental management.
(c) A set of works, projects, and activities carried out in an ecological region.
(d) Projects to be conducted in areas where possible residual, synergic, or accumulative impacts could cause destruction, isolation, or fragmentation of ecosystems.

143. In the case of the 'particular modality', according to Article 12 of the Regulations for the EIA, the environmental impact statement must contain the following:

(1) general data about the project, promoter, and responsible person for the environmental impact study;
(2) a description of the project;
(3) linkage of the project with the legal systems applicable in environmental matters and with land-use regulations;
(4) a description of the environmental system and identification of the environmental problems detected in the influence area of the project;
(5) identification, description, and evaluation of environmental impacts;
(6) preventive measures and mitigation of the environmental impacts;
(7) environmental forecasts and evaluation of alternatives; and
(8) identification of the methodological and technical elements that underpin the information indicated in the previous sections.

144. In consonance with Article 13 of the Regulations for the EIA, the regional environmental impact statement shall contain the following information:

(1) general data about the project, promoter, and responsible person for the environmental impact study;
(2) a description of the works or activities and of the programmes or partial plans of development;
(3) linkage of the project with the instruments of planning and legal systems applicable;

(4) a description of the regional environmental system and of trends of development and deterioration of the region;
(5) identification, description, and evaluation of the cumulative and residual environmental impacts on the regional environmental system;
(6) strategies for prevention and mitigation of cumulative and residual environmental impacts on the regional environmental system;
(7) regional environmental forecasts and valuation of alternatives; and
(8) identification of the methodological and technical elements that underpin the results of the manifestation of the environmental impact

145. In addition, as mentioned in line with Article 30 of the Environmental Act, in the case of activities considered highly risky, the environmental impact statement must include the study of risk. This article is complemented by Articles 17 and 18 of the Regulations for the EIA, which establish the following:

> Article 17: The developer must submit to the Ministry of the Environment the application for approval in the field of environmental impact, attaching
>
> I. The environmental impact statement;
>
> II. A summary of the content of the environmental impact statement, presented in electronic format; and
>
> III. A copy of the record of the payment of rights.
>
> In the case of activities highly risky in terms of the law, it should include a study of risk.
>
> Article 18: The study of risk referenced by the previous article will incorporate into the environmental impact statement the following information:
>
> I. Scenarios and preventive measures resulting from the analysis of the environmental risks related to the project;
>
> II. A description of the protection zones around the facilities; and
>
> III. Identification of the security measures to be taken in environmental matters.

The Ministry of the Environment has published, in the Official Journal of the Federation and in the Ecological Gazette, guides to facilitate the presentation and delivery of the study of risk.

V. The Procedure for the Environmental Impact Assessment

146. The procedure for the EIA is divided into three stages: (1) integration of the administrative dossier, (2) the EIA of the work or activity by the Ministry of Environment, and (3) the issuance of the resolution.

A. Integration of the Dossier

147. The procedure for the EIA starts with the submission of an application from those interested in carrying out works and activities subject to the EIA by the Environmental Act (Article 17 of the Regulations for the EIA), but this application must be accompanied by a technical document called an 'environmental impact statement' (EIS) (Article 30 of the Environmental Act).

148. In some cases, the EIA procedure starts with a request from the Authority. An example of such a case is when the interested party submits to the Authority a preventive report with the objective of obtaining a resolution exempting the work or activity from the procedure for the EIA and the Authority decides that the work or activity in question is not within the scope of Article 31 of the Environmental Act and, therefore, it must be submitted through the environmental impact statement procedure (Article 31, paragraph 2 of the Environmental Act).

149. Another example is the case envisaged in the last paragraph of Article 28 of the Environmental Act, conforming to which, in the cases described in section XIII of that article, the Ministry of the Environment shall notify the interested party of its intent to subject the project to the procedure of the EIA, explaining the reasons that justify such decision.

150. In any case, the purpose of both the Authority and the individual or Corporation requesting the commencement of the EIA is the integration of an administrative dossier. For this purpose, in accordance with the Regulations for the EIA, the application for approval in the field of environmental impact, its annexes, and any additional information must be submitted in electronic form and accompanied by four hard copies of its content (Article 19).

151. In accordance with Article 20 of the Regulations for the EIA, the Ministry of the Environment, when receiving the request and its annexes can communicate to the applicant the existence of formal deficiencies that can be corrected at that time. However, it may not reject any request in the terms of Article 43 of the Federal Law on Administrative Procedure. This provision holds:

> In no case administrative offices in charge of receipting documents are allowed to reject any petition.

152. So, once the request for evaluation of EIS has been received by the environmental authority, it is obliged to integrate the dossier within the following ten days (Article 35 of the Environmental Act and Article 21 of the Regulations on EIA).

153. Within that period, the Authority carries out a documentation revision process merely for verifying that the application conforms to the formalities of the law, regulations, and applicable Official Mexican Norms (OMNs).

154. Neither the law nor the Regulations for the EIA mention the consequences of a request's lacking any of the requirements specified in Article 17 of the same Regulations – in other words, if the request is not accompanied by: (a) the environmental impact statement, (b) a summary of the content of the environmental impact statement, submitted electronically, (c) a stamped copy of the payment of royalties, and (d) the study of risk; or if the information is not submitted according to the terms of Article 19; if the environmental impact statement does not satisfy the provisions of Articles 12 and 13 of the Regulation for EIA; or if the study of risk is not produced according to the terms of Article 18 of the Regulations. However, the Authority may decide not to process the dossier and, thus, not to continue with the procedure of the EIA.

155. Legislation has failed to indicate whether the Authority should or should not communicate this last fact to the petitioner, which is certainly an important legal gap, given that the petitioner likely considers that because he or she has initiated an administrative procedure, he or she should not remain ignorant of the fact that the dossier has not been processed.

156. However, a case of non-compliance with the necessary requirements, which can lead to the dossier's not being processed, should not be confused with a case of a request for additional information. This last scenario occurs when the Authority requires additional elements for evaluation and not when the dossier triggers some legal requirement.

157. Once the dossier is processed, the procedure of evaluation continues through three avenues that operate in parallel: the technical and scientific evaluation, the notification to local governments, and the public consultation.

B. Evaluation of the File

1. Technical Evaluation

158. The revision of the content of the file by the Authority concludes with the processing of the dossier and is followed by the environmental evaluation. Article 35 of the Environmental Act establishes the rules governing the assessment of the EIA by the Authority, as follows:

(a) The Ministry of the Environment shall evaluate the EIA in consonance with the Environmental Act, the Regulations for the EIA, and the OMNs, as well as the urban development programmes and ecological zoning plans of the territory, the declarations of protected natural areas, and other applicable legal provisions.
(b) The Ministry of the Environment should assess the potential effects of such works or activities on the ecosystems in question.

159. In addition, the Regulations for the EIA set forth the following rules:

(a) The Ministry of the Environment may request, in the terms laid down in the Federal Act on Administrative Procedure, the technical opinion of some unit or entity of the Federal Public Administration, when required because of the type of work or activity (Article 24).
(b) The Ministry of the Environment may consult with groups of experts when, because of the complexity or specialty of the project; it considers that their opinions can provide better elements for the formulation of the resolution (Article 24).
(c) The Ministry of the Environment must include in the file: I. the additional information that is generated; II. the technical views that had been requested; III. the comments and observations made by the interested parties in the process of public consultation, as well as the extract of the project that during that process has been published; IV. the resolution; V. the guarantees; and VI. the amendments to the project that have been made (Article 26).

2. Notification to the States

160. In the case of the works and activities referred to by sections IV, VIII, IX, and XI of Article 28 of the Environmental Act, the Ministry of the Environment shall notify the State and municipal governments or the Mexico`s City government[27], as appropriate, that it has received the environmental impact statement, so that they can express their opinions and comments (Article 33 of the Environmental Act)

3. Right to Information and Public Participation

161. In line with Article 34 of the Environmental Act, once the Ministry of the Environment has received the environmental impact statement and has processed the dossier, in accordance with Article 35, it is obliged to make the dossier available for the public. In addition, the Ministry of the Environment, upon request of any person of the community in question, may carry out a public consultation. The Regulations for the EIA govern, in Articles 40, 41, and 42, the public consultation procedure.

C. Decision by the Ministry of the Environment

162. The procedure for the EIA concludes with the issuance of an administrative decision by the Authority.

27. In 2016 the Mexican constitution was amended to modify the political status of the Federal District that used to be not considered as a state member of the Mexican Federation. In concordance with this amendment, the forma name of Federal District changed by Mexico City. However, word wide Federal District was known as Mexico City. DOF 29 Jan. 2016.

1. The Deadline for Issuing the Decision

163. Article 35*bis*[28] of the Environmental Act stipulates that a decision must be made within sixty days after an application has been filed. However, there are two cases in which this term can be modified:

(1) when there is a suspension of the procedure under which the Ministry of the Environment requests clarification or extensions of information; and
(2) when necessary because of the complexity and the dimensions of a work or activity.

164. In the first case, in terms of Article 22 of the Regulations for the EIA, the suspension of the procedure can be decreed only once and within forty days after the application has been filed when the environmental impact statement has inadequacies that make impossible the evaluation of the project until more detailed information is provided by the applicant. In this case, the term of the resolution is suspended until the petition for information is fulfilled. Article 22 stipulates:

> In cases in which the environmental impact statement has inadequacies that make impossible the evaluation of the project, the Ministry of the Environment may request the developer, for one time and within forty days from the integration of the dossier, clarifications, corrections, or extensions to the content of it and, in that case, it can suspend the term of sixty days referred to in Article 35A of the Law.

165. The suspension of the procedure may not exceed sixty days from the day on which it was declared. After this period, if the developer does not submit the requested information, the Ministry of the Environment may declare the revocation of the procedure pursuant to Article 60 of the Federal Law of Administrative Procedure.

166. It should be noted that paragraph 2 of Article 22 of the Regulations for the EIA provides in the administrative field the exact observance of the provisions of Article 35A of the Environmental Act by saying:

> The Ministry of the Environment may request clarification, corrections, or extensions to the content of the environmental impact statement submitted to it, suspending the term to conclude the procedure. In any case, the suspension may not exceed sixty days from the time that it is declared by the Ministry of the Environment, and provided that the required information is submitted.

167. The second scenario, in which the modification of the deadline to issue the final decision operates, is when – conforming to the terms of Article 46 of the Regulations for the EIA – because of the magnitude and complexity of the work or activity, it is justifiable for the Authority to take a longer period to decide, this period will be 120 days.

28. . By constitutional reform this article was added. DOF, 13 Dec. 1996.

2. The Content of the Decision

168. Article 35 of the Environmental Act notes that the Authority may decide on a petition in three different ways:

(i) By authorizing the realization of the work or activity in question, in the requested terms;

(ii) By authorizing with conditions the work or activity in question; or

(iii) By denying the requested authorization.

169. In the last case, the Environmental Act establishes only three cases for which the Authority can decide in the negative (Article 35, section III):

(a) when the work or activity is contrary to established by-laws, regulations, the OMNs, or any other applicable provisions;
(b) when the work or activity in question can result in one or more species being declared as endangered or threatened with extinction or when it affects one of these species; or
(c) when false information has been provided by the applicants with respect to the environmental impacts of the work or activity in question.

170. Given that in line with Article 28 of Environmental Act the objective of EIA is to establish the conditions that will govern the realization of works or activities that may cause ecological imbalance or may surpass the limits and conditions set up by the applicable provisions to protect the environment and to preserve and to restore the ecosystems; usually, the Authority's decision is issued in the sense of authorizing the work or activity but under certain environmental conditions.

3. The Guarantees for Compliance with the Conditions

171. Article 35 of the Environmental Act stipulates that 'the Ministry of the Environment may require the granting of insurance or guarantees regarding the fulfilment of the conditions set forth by the authorization, in the cases expressed in the Regulations for the EIA, when, during the realization of the works, serious damage to ecosystems may be caused'.

§2. Environmental Standards

172. Standards have played a very important role in environmental law and policy in Mexico since 1988, when the Environmental Act went into force, given that many aspects of environmental regulation have been developed through standards.

173. However, standards do not exclusively address environmental protection. This regulatory method was introduced almost simultaneously in the Mexican legal system by the Federal Act of Metrology and Standardization (the Standardization Act) and by the Environmental Act, both passed in 1988. However, the Environmental Act referred to standards as being specifically related to environmental protection using the term *technical ecological norms*, while the Standardization Act referred to standards in a broader sense, embracing the regulation of almost all the areas of economic activity and using the term OMNs.

174. The first difference between the OMNs and the technical ecological norms (TENs) consisted in that, whereas the 0MNs had a compulsory character, the TENs did not. This meant that while the standards were obligatory in other areas of economic activity, in the field of environmental protection, they were voluntary. However, this characteristic was not unusual because environmental legislation did not have real applications during the period 1988–1992. On the other hand, neither the Environmental Act nor the Standardization Act regulated the process of the elaboration of standards.

175. In 1992, a new Standardization Act was passed by the Federal Congress. It introduced two innovations. First, this Law established a procedure for the elaboration of standards and, second, it introduced the distinction between OMNs and Mexican norms (MNs).

176. According to the new Act, both OMNs and MNs are considered standards that establish rules, specifications, attributes, test methods, guides, characteristics, or prescriptions related to products, processes, facilities, systems, activities, services, or production methods or operations, as well as rules regarding labelling, marking, terminology, symbols, and packaging. However, their approval processes are different.

177. MNs are elaborated by Normalization Organizations or by the Ministry who is competent in the specific area to which the norm will be applicable. (Article 3, section X) These kinds of standards are not published in the *Federal Official Journal*.

178. On the other hand, OMNs are projected by the Ministry responsible for the control or regulation of the products, methods, processes or activities or areas that will be regulated by the norm; however, they should be approved by the National Advisory Committees of Normalization, which are composed of technical 'personnel competent in the matter that corresponds to the committee and to industrial organizations; lenders of services; merchants; agricultural, forest, or fishing producers; centres of scientific or technological research; professional schools; and consumers'. This class of standards should be published in the *Federal Official Journal* as a condition of validity.

179. In both cases, participation of regulated subjects in the elaboration process plays an important role, because they are part of the Normalization Organizations as well as the National Advisory Committees that approve the standards. Besides the projects of OMNs should be submitted to public consultation by the government. Thus, in a way, standards are mechanisms of self-regulation.

180. Another difference between OMNs and MNs is that the OMNs are mandatory, while MNs are voluntary. However, should an OMN remit to the fulfilment of an MN, it becomes compulsory as well.

181. It is important to mention that in 1992, all the technical ecological norms promulgated under the Environmental Act transformed into OMNs and, therefore, they acquired a mandatory character. Furthermore, in 1996, the Environmental Act included OMNs as an environmental policy instrument, pointing out their specific objectives (Article 36) and establishing their mandatory character (Article 37*bis*); it also mentioned some principles for their elaboration (Article 37). Article 36 of the Environmental Act established that OMNs objectives are to:

> I. Establish the requirements, specifications, conditions, procedures, goals, parameters and permissible limits that will be observed in regions, areas, basins, or ecosystems, in uses of natural resources, in the development of economic activities, in the uses and destination of goods, in inputs, and in processes;
>
> II. Considering necessary conditions for people's wellbeing, natural resource preservation and environmental protection;
>
> III. Encourage or induce economic agents to reorient their processes and technologies for environmental protection and sustainable development;
>
> IV. Provide long-term certainty for investment and induce economic agents to assume the cost of environmental involvement rise; and
>
> V. Promoting productive activities in a framework of efficiency and sustainability.

182. In the same vain, Federal Law on Metrology and Standardization grants to OMNs a clearly regulatory character when pointing out in Article 40 that:

> The Official Mexican Norms will have as purpose to set forth:
>
> I. The characteristics or specifications that the products and processes should gather when these can constitute a risk for the security of people or damage to human health, fauna, flora, the environment, or the preservation of natural resources;
>
> II. The characteristics or specifications of the products used as matter or parts or materials for the production or assembly of final products subject to the execution of official Mexican norms, whenever to complete the specifications of these, they plows indispensable those of this matter, parts, or materials;
>
> III. The characteristics or specifications that should govern the services when these can constitute a risk for the security of people or damage to human health,

animals, plants, or the environment or when they relate to the benefit of services in a widespread way for the consumer;

IV. The characteristics or specifications related to instruments of measure, measurement patterns and methods, verification, calibration, and traceability;

V. The container specifications or procedures and packing of the products that constitute a risk to the security of people or damage the health of same or the environment;

VI. (repealed.);

VII. The conditions of health, security, and hygiene that will be observed in the work centres and other public centres of meeting;

VIII. The nomenclature, expressions, abbreviations, symbols, diagrams, or drawings that will be used in the industrial, technical, or commercial language of services or of communication;

IX. The description of emblems, symbols, and countersigns for ends of this Law;

X. The characteristics or specifications, approaches, and procedures that protect and promote the improvement of the environment and the ecosystems, as well as the preservation of natural resources;

XI. The characteristics or specifications, approaches, and procedures that protect, and promote the health of people, animals, or plants;

XII. The determination of commercial, sanitary, and ecological information of quality, security, and hygiene and requirements that should complete the labels, containers, packing, and publicity of the products and services to provide information to the consumer or user;

XIII. The characteristics or specifications that should govern the teams, materials, and devices of industrial and commercial facilities; of services and servants for sanitary ends; of agriculture, cattle, and ecology; of communications, security, or quality, and particularly when they are dangerous;

XIV. (repealed.);

XV. The support of the origin denominations for products of the country;

XVI. The characteristics and/or specifications that should govern the apparatus, nets, and communication systems, as well as vehicles of transport, teams, and related services to protect the general roads of communication and the security of their users;

XVII. The characteristics or specifications, approaches, and procedures for the handling, transport, and disposition of materials and dangerous industrial residuals and of radioactive substances; and

XVIII. Others those are required to normalize products, methods, processes, systems, or industrial, practical, commercial services in conformity with other legal dispositions, whenever Articles 45 and 47 govern them.

183. The criteria, rules, instructions books, hand books, procedures, or other dispositions of mandatory character that dependences are required to establish in regards of the matters and purposes that are set forth in this article must be issued as official Mexican norms conforming to the procedure set forth in this Law.

184. On the other hand, section I of Article 36 of the Environmental Act establishes that, among other objectives, OMNs 'establish the requirements, specifications, conditions, procedures, goals, parameters, and permissible limits that will be observed in regions, areas, basins, or ecosystems, in the uses of natural resources, in the development of economic activities, in the uses and destinations of goods, in inputs, and in processes'.

§3. Environmental Licences

185. Polluting activities are subject to different permits. Air pollutant emissions from fixed sources subject to federal jurisdiction require of an operation licence in agreement with Articles 111*bis* of Environment Act and 18 of the Regulation for

Prevention and Control of Air Pollution,[29] whereas in most of the cities air pollutant emissions from vehicles are required to pass the certification of emissions tests granted by local governments.

186. In accordance to Article 88 of National Waters Act, water pollutant discharge to national water bodies require of a discharge permit.[30] Finally, as stated by Articles 46, 47, and 48 of General Waste Act and 152 of Environmental Act, grate hazardous waste generators[31] need to report to the Environmental Authority the type and amount of hazardous waste generated by them.

187. Since the middle of the 1990s, the Ministry of the Environment has been trying to integrate all such permits – including the environmental impact authorization – into a unique environmental licence.

188. . Aimed at such objective, in 1996, the Federal Congress approved an amendment to the Environmental Act to include Articles 35*bis* 3, 109*bis*, and 109*bis* 1.

189. As stated by Article 35*bis* 3, the Ministry of the Environment, upon request by the promoter, will integrate with the environmental impact authorization the other permissions, licences, and authorizations under its jurisdiction. In addition, Article 109*bis* holds that the Ministry of the Environment shall integrate an inventory of waste, air, and water emissions under Federal jurisdiction, as well as a comprehensive system of environmental information based on the permits and licences granted by it.

190. Finally, Article 109*bis* 1 establishes that the Secretariat shall set up the necessary mechanisms and procedures for the interested parties to obtain, through a single procedure, all permits, licences, or authorizations that must be granted by the Ministry of the Environment.

---

29. According to Art. 111*bis* of Environmental Law, the following are considered fixed sources of federal jurisdiction: chemical, petroleum, and petrochemical industries, paints and inks, automotive, pulp and paper, metallurgy, glass, electric power generation, industry of asbestos, cement and lime, and treatment of hazardous waste.
30. Fifth Paragraph of Art. 27 of the Mexican Federal Constitution listed those water bodies that are considered as national property. The list includes: waters of territorial sea in the extension and under the terms set forth by International Law; over internal waters; waters of lagoons and estuaries permanently or intermittently connecting with the sea; those of natural inland lakes which are directly connected with streams constantly flowing; river waters and their direct and indirect tributaries, from the site of the riverbed where the first permanent, intermittent, or torrential waters start to flow, to their mouth in the sea, lakes, lagoons, or estuaries owned by the nation; those of constant or intermittent streams and their direct or indirect tributaries, whenever their beds along all the length of its way or in a portion thereof serve as a boundary line of national land territory or between two States, or when they flow from one State to another or cross the Republic's boundary line; those of lakes, lagoons, or estuaries whose beds, zones, or streams are crossed by boundary lines dividing one or more States or between the Republic and a neighbouring country, or when the stream shoreline serves as a boundary between two States or between the Republic and a neighbouring country; those of springs flowing from beaches, maritime areas, streams, basins, river beds, banks of lakes, lagoons, or estuaries owned by the Nation, and the ones extracted from mines; and the streams, beds, or banks of lakes and interior streams in the extensions established by the Law.
31. According to Art. 5, s. XII of the Waste Act, Great Generator: A person or company that generates an amount equal to or greater than 10 tons. In total gross weight of waste per year or its equivalent in another unit of measurement.

191. In the same vein, in 2004 the Regulation under LGEEPA regarding to the Register of emissions and transference of pollutants was published in the *Federal Official Journal.* In line with the new Regulation, all sources of pollution subjected to federal jurisdiction are obliged to report to the Ministry of the Environment their emission and transference of pollutant to air, water, soil, subsoil, hazardous materials, and waste on annual basis.

§4. Environmental Audits

192. In 1996, the Environmental Act was amended to introduce a section focused on self-regulation and on the environmental audits integrated by Articles 38, 38*bis*, 38*bis* 1, and 38*bis* 2, and on 29 April 2010 the new Regulation under the Environmental Act regarding self-regulation and environmental audits was published in the *Federal Official Journal.*[32] Environmental audits may be a more effective method to improve the environmental performance of companies than inspection and monitoring, but a scenario where the environmental authority waives its obligation to apply the Law and becomes a mere promoter of its fulfilment is not possible according to the provisions of the Political Constitution of the United Mexican States.

193. In accordance with Article 38*bis* of the Environmental Act, the environmental audit allows those in charge of the operation of a company to voluntarily carry out a methodological examination of their operations with respect to the pollution and the risk that they generate, as well as of the level of compliance with environmental regulations and the international parameters and of good practices of applicable operation and engineering, with the intention of defining the necessary preventive and corrective measures to protect the environment.

194. The Ministry of Environment plays an important role in environmental audits. Paragraph 2 of Article 38*bis* establishes that the Ministry of the Environment will develop programmes intended to stimulate the accomplishment of environmental audits and mentions that the Ministry shall supervise their realization.

195. Those conducting environmental audits are legible to obtain the certificate of clean industry. The clean industry certificate is a document granted by the Attorney General's Office for Environmental Protection to those industries that have satisfactorily implemented the plan of action derived from an environmental audit. Nevertheless, this certificate does not grant any type of legal advantage over other companies that have not conducted an environmental audit, but simply a greater social acceptance and a better position in the market. Article 28 of the LGEEPA Regulations on Self-Regulation and Environmental Audits states:

> Article 28. In consideration of the activity carried out by the Companies, the Certificate issued by the Attorney General's Office shall have the following modalities:

32. However, the origins of the environmental audit in Mexico go back to 1992 when Attorney General Office for environmental Protection was created and within this a Deputy Attorney General in charge of this function. *See* the Agreement that regulates the organization and internal functioning of INE and PROFEPA published in the DOF on 13 Dec. 1996.

I. Clean industry: for works and activities of the industrial sector;

II. Tourism environmental quality: for tourism sector activities and services, and

III. Environmental quality: for those activities not contemplated in the two previous fractions.

Each of these modalities will have different levels of Environmental Performance, according to the established in the Terms of Reference and based on this will be granted the corresponding Certificate.

The Certificates will have a validity of two years counted from its notification.

196. Despite the voluntary nature of the environmental audit, the administrative authority plays an important role in the regulatory process derived from environmental auditing for a variety of reasons.

197. First, the second paragraph of Article 38*bis* states that the Ministry of the Environment will develop a programme aimed at stimulating the performance of environmental audits and mentions that, in its case, the aforementioned unit will supervise its execution whit that purpose:

I. Will elaborate the terms of reference that establish the methodology for the accomplishment of the environmental audits;

II. Establish a system of approval and accreditation of environmental experts and auditors, determining the procedures and requirements that must be met by interested parties to join the system, and, if applicable, comply with the provisions of the Law on Metrology and Standardization.

To this end, a technical committee composed of representatives of research institutions, colleges and professional associations and organizations of the industrial sector will be integrated;

III. Develop training programs in the area of expertise and environmental audits;

IV. It will implement a recognition and stimulus system that allows to identify the industries that fulfil in a timely manner the commitments acquired in the environmental audits;

V. Promote the creation of regional centres to support the medium and small industry, in order to facilitate the performance of audits in these sectors, and

VI. It will be agreed or with physical or moral persons, public or private, to carry out environmental audits.

198. Second, in accordance with Articles 2, sections I and 33 of the Regulations under the Environmental Act on Self-Regulation and Environmental Audit, the entities responsible for conducting the environmental audit have the character of *verification units*, that is, to say of bodies whose power of verification is granted by the authority in terms of Articles 68 of the Law on Metrology and Standardization and 87 of its Regulations.

199. Third, in accordance with Articles 15 and 16 of the LGEEPA Regulations, the environmental authority is aware of the outcome of the environmental audit.

200. Finally, based on the audit report, the environmental authority decides whether to grant the corresponding certificate.

201. Because of this hybrid character, conducting environmental audits frequently leads to a conflict between the authority's obligation to apply the Law through the inspection and monitoring procedure and the voluntary commitment assumed with the polluting sources to carry out the Action plan derived from an environmental audit.

202. Therefore, environmental audits involve a certain level of secret agreement between regulated subjects and the authority to break the law without facing the consequences.

203. To avoid this irregular appearance, environmental audits should focus on those areas of environmental protection where the government does not have sufficient information to issue regulations and where private actors have sufficient information, capacity, and experience to self-regulate.

204. Finally, although the LGEEPA chapter subject to analysis refers to both environmental audits and self-regulation, this last aspect is not developed in the Law or in its Regulations, since it is exclusively identified with environmental auditing, Which, as we have seen, does not have that character of self-regulation but it is a process of certification.

Chapter 2. Air Pollution

205. In general, air pollution has been a constant concern for the Mexican government. At the beginning of the twentieth century, the air pollution issue was addressed from the perspective of private law, as, for example, with the Civil Federal Code of 1928, which prohibited the construction of chimneys near adjacent properties. It also prescribed minimum distances at which chimneys had to be set back from adjoining properties.

206. The government then addressed the pollution problem as a public health issue. This resulted in the enactment of the Regulations for Dangerous, Disgusting, and Unhealthy Industrial or Commercial Facilities of 1940, which established that the air emissions from these facilities: (a) should be channelled through chimneys with an altitude of at least 5 m above the highest building in around 6 m, and (b) should not contain more than 13 million/m^3 of pollutant particles.

207. In 1971, Article 73 of the Mexican Federal Constitution was amended to add section XVI, which empowered the National Council of General Health to adopt measures to prevent and to combat environmental pollution. In the same year, the Federal Act to Control and Prevent Environmental Pollution was enacted. Like the 1940 Regulations, this Law focused on the effects of air pollution on human health.

208. Conforming to the Federal Act to Control and Prevent Environmental Pollution, emitting, or discharging pollutants that could affect human life and health, flora and fauna, and natural resources in general was prohibited. This Law ruled that all sources of pollution (industries and vehicles) must have a licence granted by the Federal Environmental Authority and must comply with the limits of pollutant emissions established by the Regulations. A regulation of this Act established the parameters of emissions from pollutant sources, and many standards were developed to regulate the emission of: (a) solid particles, (b) humidity, (c) SO^2, (d) CO^2, (e) CO, (f) oxygen present in combustion gases, and (g) SO^3, among other gases.

209. In 1982, the Federal Act for Environmental Protection repealed by the Federal Act to Control and Prevent Environmental Pollution. No fundamental changes were introduced by the new Law to deal with air pollution. Nevertheless, during the time in which it was in force, new standards related to pollution emissions were approved.

210. As mentioned in Part I of this book, in 1987, The Federal Constitution was amended to incorporate the concurrent jurisdictions system that empowered both the Federal and local governments to legislate on environmental protection. Under this rule, in 1988, the Ecological Equilibrium and Environmental Protection General Act was passed, and the thirty-one States of the Mexican Federation as well as the government of Mexico City approved local environmental laws.

211. These actions changed the governmental approach to dealing with pollution, as they focused not only on air pollution and its effects on human health, but also on the protection of the environment as a whole and on the impacts of all kinds of pollution on human health as well as on natural resources. The Environmental Act regulates air pollution from both fixed sources and mobile sources.

212. According to the Environmental Act, the biggest industrial sources of air pollution were considered to be under Federal jurisdiction, whereas vehicles and medium- and small-sized industrial and commercial sources of air pollution were considered to be under local jurisdiction.

213. The Environmental Act points out that the following are considered to be fixed sources under Federal jurisdiction: chemical industries, petroleum and petrochemistry, paints and inks, cellulose and paper, metallurgy, glass, electric power generation, asbestos, cement plants, calera and treatment of dangerous wastes. Consequently, any other fixed sources of atmospheric contamination are considered to be under local jurisdiction (Article 111*bis*, penultimate paragraph).

214. The prevention and control of atmospheric contamination generated by fixed or mobile sources of local jurisdiction correspond to local governments and to the municipalities where these are located in the following way:

(a) The prevention and control of air pollution generated by fixed sources that work as industrial establishments, as well as by mobile sources that are not under Federal jurisdiction, (Article 7, section III) correspond to the States and the Federal District.
(b) The application of legal provisions regarding the prevention and control of air pollution generated by fixed sources considered to be mercantile or service establishments, as well as those emissions of pollutants coming from mobile sources that are not considered to be under Federal jurisdiction, corresponds to municipalities (Article 8, section III).

§1. Pollution Coming from Fixed Sources

215. First, Article 110 of the Environmental Act points out a series of principles that govern public policies in regard to air protection. These principles are the following:

- The quality of the air should be satisfactory in all the human settlements and the regions of the country.
- Air pollutant emissions from natural or artificial sources must be reduced and controlled to reach a satisfactory air quality for the population's well-being, as well as for the ecological balance.

216. However, neither the Environmental Act nor the local environmental laws have established specific obligations to reduce pollutant emissions, but only to control them. The Environmental Act established four mechanisms to deal with air pollution from industries:

(a) all industrial sources of air pollution must obtain a licence of operation granted by the Federal Environmental Authority;
(b) equipment and systems to control emissions must be installed by polluters;
(c) all industrial sources of air pollution have to integrate their inventory of emissions; and

(d) all industrial sources of air pollution must install monitoring systems.

217. The Regulations under the Environmental Act in the area of Prevention and Control of Pollution of 1988 (as amended in 2004) sets up the general rule according to which: 'emissions of odours, gases, as well as solid particles to air by fixed sources shall not exceed the maximum permissible levels of emissions that by pollutants or by sources are established by the Ministry of Environment in cooperation with the Ministry of Public Health' (Article 16). It also established the following obligations for fixed sources of pollution under Federal jurisdiction:

(a) To integrate an inventory of air pollutant emissions, to measure them and to register their results in the formats that the Ministry of the Environment determines and to remit this registration when requested to do so by such agency (Article 17, section II).
(b) To annually present the certificate of operation to upgrade the information that the fixed source of pollution presented with the application of the licence referred to by Article 111bis of the Environmental Act (Article 21).
(c) To have a register of operations and maintenance of the control of equipment that produces pollution (Article 17, section VI).
(d) To use equipment and control systems for air emissions so that these do not surpass the maximum permissible levels set forth by the corresponding OMNs (Article 17, section I).
(e) To instal platforms and monitoring ports (Article 17, section III).
(f) To carry out the monitoring of air pollutant emissions when the source is in urban or suburban areas, when it is adjacent to natural protected areas and when their operation or characteristics can cause serious deterioration to ecosystems (Article 17, section V).
(g) To give prior notice to the Secretary at the beginning of the operation of processes in the case of programmed shutdowns and immediately in cases for which these are incidental, if they can result in contamination (Article 17, section VII).
(h) To give immediate warning to the Ministry of the Environment in the case of a flaw in the control equipment, so that this determines the conducive action, if the flaw can result in contamination (Article 17, section VIII).
(i) To channel the emissions of air pollutants that are generated by fixed sources of Federal jurisdiction through ducts or chimneys, which will have the effective necessary height, in accordance with the corresponding OMNs, to disperse pollutant emissions (Articles 23 and 24).
(j) To maintain, under conditions of security, platforms, and monitoring ports and to maintain the gauging of measuring equipment (Article 26).

218. Control of air pollution coming from other fixed sources not included in the list of Article 111*bis* of the Law corresponds to local governments.

§2. Pollution Coming from Mobile Sources

219. Federal legislation, in practice, is not in charge of the prevention and control of air pollution coming from mobile sources. Although the Regulations under the Environmental Act regarding Prevention and Control of Pollution Generated by Vehicles Circulating in the Federal District and the Metropolitan Area was issued in 1988, its provisions are not in force, because, in 1993, a Constitutional Amendment granted to the Legislative Assembly of the Federal District the ability to enact its own local environmental law, which in fact recaptures the content of such Regulations.

220. The main instrument to deal with air pollution coming from mobile sources is the verification of the pollutant emissions of vehicles that are governed by several States of the country, as well as the circulation restriction that is applied exclusively in the metropolitan area of Mexico City.

221. The Environmental Act tries to control air pollution from vehicles and other mobile sources through the establishment of emission standards. In fact, further details to the Environmental Act's provisions in this area were set forth by two Regulations to this Act enacted in 1988.

222. One of these Regulations was designed to deal with air pollution from industries and vehicles in the entire national territory. The main objective of this Regulation was to control but not to reduce the polluting emissions by establishing standards of emission. Nevertheless, this Regulation also set up the basis for building a national inventory of emissions.

223. The second Regulation that was exclusively designed to deal with polluting emissions from vehicles operating in the metropolitan area of Mexico City provided support for two environmental strategies: (a) standards that establish stricter levels of pollutant emissions; and (b) the *Hoy no circula* programme, which prohibits the use of vehicles that do not comply with the emission standards for the roads.

224. Ironically, this approach had more negative than positive effects on the air quality of Mexico City, as there was an increase in the number of vehicles on the road instead of a decrease in pollution. This happened because the *Hoy no circula* programme did not include tax considerations, and consequently, despite the stricter standards regulating emissions from vehicles, the number of cars increased after the establishment of this programme.

§3. Climate Change

225. In 2012, the General Law of Climate Change was passed by the Federal Congress.[33] Even when the general objective of this law is to set up the legal frame to deal with negative effects of climate change, it did not repeal the Environmental Law provisions regarding to air pollution.

226. In Accordance with its Article 2, this Law pursues a number of specific goals, among others:

(a) To regulate greenhouse gas emissions.

33. DOF, 06 Jun. 2012.

(b) To regulate actions aimed at mitigating of and adapting to climate change.
(c) To reduce population and ecosystems vulnerability.
(d) To promote transition to a competitive, sustainable, and low carbon emissions economy.

227. To get these objectives, the Law establishes the following legal instruments:

(a) The National Strategy of Climate Change, the Programme of Climate Change, and the local programmes on Climate Change.
(b) The National Inventory of anthropogenic emissions and abortion by basins.
(c) The National System of Information on Climate Change.
(d) The Climate Change Fund.
(e) The register of emissions by mobile and fix sources.
(f) Economic Instruments.
(g) OMNs.

228. Like all environmental laws, this Law establishes the concurrence of the three orders of government in the application of the measures regarding to mitigation, adaptation, and vulnerability reduction in a balanced manner. Among the main environmental policy instruments established by the Law are the following:

a) The National Climate Change System (SNCC) is constituted as a permanent mechanism of concurrence, communication, collaboration, coordination, and coordination of the three orders of government, as well as the private sector and the social sector.

b) As part of the SNCC, the Inter-Ministerial Commission on Climate Change is created.

c) The Climate Change Council is created.

d) The National Institute of Ecology and Climate Change is created as a decentralized public agency of the Federal Public Administration. Consequently, the current National Institute of Ecology disappears.

229. 229. Notwithstanding the foregoing, it is a purely programmatic law that duplicates the content of the Environmental Law in the field of air pollution, and does not establish any specific regulations on mitigation and adaptation to climate change.

Article 87 of the General Climate Change Law compels the Ministry of the Environment to create the Register of emissions generated by mobile and fixed sources (Article 87) that are considered as subject to be obliged to report. In complement of such provision, Article 88 of the mentioned Law obliged corporations and persons responsible for fixed sources subject to report to provide the Ministry of Environment with the necessary information, data, and documents about their emissions in order to integrate the Register mentioned by Article 87.

230. On the other hand, in 2014 the Regulation under Climate Change Law on National Register of Emissions was published.[34] This is basically a regulation under Article 87 of the General Climate Change Law, in this way. Indeed, Article 1 of the Regulation states that:

This Regulation is one of the general observance in all the national territory and has the object of regulating the Law in regard to the National Register of Emissions; its enforcement corresponds to the Federal Executive through the Ministry (of the Environment), without detriment of the faculties of other Offices of the Federal Executive.

231. To meet this goal, first, the Regulation lists in Article 3 those economic sectors and those activities that are considers as sites subject to report.

232. Finally, Article 5 identifies those greenhouse gases and compounds subject to report.

233. However, Registration of air pollutant emissions is not just ruled by General Climate Change Law and its regulation but also by the Environmental Law and its Regulation on Emissions Registration and Transference of Pollutants published in the Official Gazette of the Federation in 2004, which regulates the provisions on the Emissions Register created in the mentioned law.[35]

234. However, unlike what happens with General Climate Change Law Regulation, this regulation deals with registration and transference of pollutant emissions to air, water, soil, subsoil, hazardous materials and waste, and other substances.

34. DOF, 28 Oct. 2014.
35. DOF, 03 Jun. 2004.

Chapter 3. Water Pollution

§1. Regulation of Water Use

235. Paragraph 1 of Article 27 of the Mexican Constitution prescribes that ownership of lands and waters within the boundaries of the national territory is vested originally in the Nation, which has had and still has the right to transmit the title thereof to private persons, thereby constituting private property. Consequently, the Mexican Constitution allows private property of water with some limitations. In this regard, Article 27 points out that:

(a) only Mexicans by birth or naturalization and Mexican companies have the right to acquire domain over lands, waters, and their appurtenances or to obtain water exploitation concessions;
(b) the State may grant the same right to foreigners, if they agree before the Ministry of Foreign Relations to consider themselves as nationals in respect to such property and not to invoke the protection of their governments about said property, under penalty, in case of defaulting on the agreement, of forfeiting in benefit of the Nation, the property acquired by virtue thereof; and
(c) in no case, may foreigners acquire direct domain over lands and waters in a zone of 100 km along the international borders and 50 km along the shore.

236. Private property of waters is not an absolute right. In agreement with paragraph 3 of Article 27, the Nation shall at all times have the right to impose on private property of waters such restrictions as the public interest may demand, as well as to regulate, for social benefit, the utilization of those waters so as to make an equitable distribution of public wealth, to conserve them, to achieve a balanced development of the country, and to improve the living conditions of rural and urban populations.

237. Consequently, Article 27 of the Mexican Constitution empowers the Nation to issue measures aimed at establishing adequate provisions, uses, reserves, and allocations of waters to carry out public works and to plan and regulate the creation, maintenance, improvement, and growth of population centres; to preserve and restore environmental balance; to provide, under the terms set forth by the Law, collective exploitation and to prevent the destruction of natural resources and damages that property may suffer to the detriment of society.

238. On the other hand, in consonance with paragraph 5 of Article 27 of the Mexican Constitution, the property of certain specific waters is vested in the Nation. This provision points out that:

> The Nation has full ownership over the waters of territorial sea in the extension and under the terms set forth by international law; internal waters; waters of lagoons and estuaries permanently or intermittently connecting with the sea; those of natural inland lakes that are directly connected with streams constantly

flowing; river waters and their direct and indirect tributaries, from the site of the riverbed where the first permanent, intermittent, or torrential waters start to flow, to their mouth in the sea; lakes, lagoons, or estuaries owned by the Nation; those of constant or intermittent streams and their direct or indirect tributaries, whenever their beds along all the length of their way or in a portion thereof serve as a boundary line of national land territory or between two States, or when they flow from one State to another or cross the Republic's boundary line; those of lakes, lagoons, or estuaries whose beds, zones, or streams are crossed by boundary lines dividing one or more States or between the Republic and a neighboring country, or when the stream shoreline serves as a boundary between two States or between the Republic and a neighboring country; those of springs flowing from beaches, maritime areas, streams, basins, riverbeds, banks of lakes, lagoons, or estuaries owned by the Nation, and the ones extracted from mines; and the streams, beds, or banks of lakes and interior streams in the extensions established by the Law.

239. In addition, paragraph 6 of Article 27 of the Mexican Constitution holds that the Nation's dominion of the aforementioned waters is inalienable and not subject to the statute of limitations, and consequently, the use or enjoyment of such waters by private persons or by companies incorporated in accordance with Mexican laws may not be undertaken except by means of concessions granted by the President of the Republic and in accordance with the rules and conditions set forth by the Laws.

240. By contrast, according to paragraph 5 of Article 27, underground waters are not considered to be national property. Thus, using and enjoining underground waters do not require a concession. That provision recognizes that such waters may be freely extracted by artificial works and may be appropriated by the owner of the land where such waters are located.

241. However, the final part of paragraph 5 of Article 27 establishes that whenever the public interest should so require it, or whenever other uses are affected, the President of the Republic may regulate the extraction and use of underground waters and may even establish banned zones, and the same may be done regarding other waters of national property. In these cases, using or enjoying underground waters by individuals or Corporations shall require a concession, as in the case of national waters.

242. Based on the above listings of the Constitution, the National Waters Act regulates the establishment of reserves of waters, regulated areas of extraction, and banned zones. The Act also regulates the administrative procedure through which the Nation grants concessions to use and enjoy national waters or underground waters in regulated or banned zones. Marine waters are regulated by the Federal Act of the Sea.

243. On the other hand, paragraph 5 of Article 27 prescribes that any other waters not included in the list above shall be considered as an integral part of the land through which they flow or where their deposits are located, but should they be located in two or more lots, the use of such waters shall be considered of public convenience and subject to provisions issued by the States. Consequently, local governments have jurisdiction to legislate on waters not included in the list of paragraph 5 of Article 27.

I. Reserves, Regulations, and Banned Zones

244. The Waters Act defines the meaning of reserved areas, regulated areas, and banned areas in the following terms:

- Reserved areas: those specific areas of aquifers, watersheds, or hydrological regions in which there have been established limitations for exploitation, use of a portion or all of the water available, with the aim of providing a public service, introducing a programme of restoration or preservation, or when the State has decided to exploit these waters for public utility reasons (National Waters Act, Article 3, section LXIV).
- Regulated areas: those specific areas of aquifers, hydrological basins, or hydrological regions that, because of their characteristics of deterioration, hydrological unbalance, risk or damage to water or the environment, fragility of ecosystems, over-exploitation, as well as to their reorganization and restoration, require specific hydro management to guarantee hydrological sustainability (National Waters Act, Article 3, section LXIII).
- Banned areas: those specific areas of hydrological regions, watersheds, or aquifers for which water uses are not allowed in addition to those legally established and that are controlled by specific regulations, undergoing deterioration of water in quantity or quality by their allocation to the hydrological, sustainability or by damage to the bodies of water on their surface and underground. (National Waters Act, Article 3, section LXV).

245. This means that reserved areas, regulated areas, and banned areas are legal institutions that do not prevent the use or enjoyment of national waters, but their use is regulated. The establishment of a regulated area limits but does not forbid the granting of concessions for the use or enjoyment of national waters.

246. For its part, the establishment of a banned area does not prohibit the granting of licences for using waters, but, in the case of ground waters, it restricts the right of free access guaranteed by paragraph 5 of Article 27 of the Constitution, cited above, whereas in the case of surface waters nationalized in the paragraph 5 of Article 27, banned areas result in the requirement of concessions for their use or exploitation by individuals.

247. Furthermore, in the case of national surface waters, the requirement of concessions is due not by the shortage of resources, but by the national character of the waters, addressed in paragraph 5 of Article 27, according to which the use of a resource under the public domain of the Nation, which is also inalienable, requires the granting of concessions.

248. In contrast, in the case of groundwater that can be freely extracted and appropriated by the landowner, a grant is required only when a banned area has been declared, because otherwise, the concession would be unnecessary.

249. Second, the National Waters Act notes general rules that apply to decrees establishing reserve areas and regulated or banned areas. Finally, it contains specific rules for issuing each one of these legal instruments.

II. Assignments and Concessions

250. The Waters Act points out in Article 1 that the objective of regulating the exploitation, use, or enjoyment of these waters, its distribution and control, as well as the preservation of its quantity and quality, is to achieve its integral sustainable development.

251. National waters are defined in Article 3 of the Waters Act as 'the waters that are the property of the Nation, in terms of paragraph 5 of Article 27 of the Mexican Constitution'. Article 16 of the Waters Act adds to the list contemplated in that Constitutional precept the residual waters coming from the use of national waters.

252. In the same vein, Article 18 of the Waters Act stipulates that the national waters of the subsoil may be freely extracted by artificial works, except when the Federal Executive for reasons of public interest regulates its extraction and its use or establishes banned areas.

253. The Waters Act refers in Title 6 to different types of uses of national waters: urban public use, agricultural use, use in electric power generation, and use in other productive activities. The Act also states in Article 20 that in all cases, exploitation, use, or enjoyment of the national waters by individuals or Corporations will be through concessions granted by the Federal Executive through the National Water Commission and that, in the case of any department or agency, decentralized public administration, or federal, State, or municipal council, use or exploitation is allowed by assignment. Extension of the rights granted by concession or assignment ranges from five to thirty years (Article 24 of the Waters Act).

254. Concessions and assignments confer an onerous use of the national waters. Pursuant to sections IV and V of Article 29 and Article *29bis* of the Waters Act, concessionaires and allocators have, among others, the obligation 'to pay duties for extraction, consumption, and use of the national waters' and 'to pay duties in accordance with the established Federal Tax Laws in force and in other applicable provisions'.

255. Reiterating this obligation, Article 112 of the Waters Act provides that the exploitation, use, or enjoyment of national waters, including those from the subsoil, will require the payment by the user of the duties established by the Federal Tax Laws.

256. In addition, Article 222 of the Federal Duties Act (FDA) stipulates that:

> Individuals and Corporations that use, exploit or enjoy national waters, either in fact or covered by titles of assignment, concession, authorization, or permission granted by the Federal government, according to the area of availability of water in which it carries out its extraction in accordance with the territorial division contained in Article 231 of this Law, are liable for payment of the duty on water.

257. A Pursuant to the transcribed Article, the payment of the duty is calculated on the basis of the volume of water allocated or exploited measured in cubic metres, while the rate is established in Article 223.

§2. Water Pollution

258. At the Federal level, pollution of national waters is regulated by the Waters Act, the Environmental Act, the LFM, the LFD, and the ONMs. These laws establish the following instruments to deal with water pollution: declarations of classification of national bodies of water, the obligation of giving treatment to water prior to its discharge, discharge permits, permits for infiltration of waters, ‘particular conditions of discharge’, limits of pollutant discharges, and payment for rights for discharge. These are described below.

I. Declaration of Classification of Bodies of Waters

259. The general instrument for regulating water pollution is constituted by the Declaration of Classification of Bodies of National Waters. However, legislation does not define this instrument, and Article 87 of the Waters Act simply points out that:

> The authority of the water shall determine the parameters that will met by the discharges, the capacity of assimilation, and the dilution that national waters have and the pollutant discharges that these can receive, as well as the parameters of quality and the terms necessary to reach them, by means of the expedition of the Declaration of Classification of Bodies of National Waters, which will be published in the Official Newspaper of the Federation.

260. The declaration shall include the following:

(1) the delimitation of the classified body of water;
(2) the parameters that will complete the discharges pursuant to the classified body of water and to the periods foreseen in the regulation of this Law;
(3) the capacity of the classified body of water to dilute and to assimilate pollutants; and
(4) the maximum limits of discharge of the analysed pollutants, based on fixing the conditions unique to the discharge.

II. The Obligation of Giving Treatment to Residual Water Discharges

261. Another general obligation regarding water pollution is established by Article 121 of the Environmental Act. As stated in this provision, no one is allowed to discharge or infiltrate into anybody or flow of water or on the ground or underground, residual waters that contain pollutants, without prior treatment and the permission or authorization granted by Federal Authority or by the local Authority in cases of discharges into waters of local jurisdiction or into municipal drainage systems and sewer systems of centres of population.

262. In addition, the General Act of Health, in Article 122, reiterates this obligation, pointing out that it is forbidden to discharge residual waters without treatment so that those discharges meet the sanitary standards enacted by the Secretary of Health to avoid risks to public health.

III. Discharge Permits

263. As stated in paragraph b of section XL of Article 3 of the Waters Act, the permit for discharge is the 'Title that the Federal Executive grants through "the Commission" or the Organization of Basins, according to their respective competences, for the discharge of residual waters in receiving bodies of national property, to individuals or to public or private Corporations.'

264. Article 88 of the Waters Act establishes that 'individuals and Corporations shall require discharge permission issued by the "Authority of the Water" to pour residual waters in permanent or intermittent ways into receiving bodies that are national waters or other property, including marine waters, as well as when they infiltrate them into lands that are national property or on other lands when they can contaminate the underground water or aquifers'. Reiterating this obligation, section I of Article 88*bis* of the Waters Act points out that individuals or Corporations that discharge residual waters into receiving bodies that are governed by law should have the discharge permission.

265. As an exemption, Article 88*bis* 1 points out that discharges of residual waters from domestic use that are not part of a municipal system or sewer system do not require permission but only have to meet the limits established by the OMNs.

266. The Environmental Act also refers to the permit for the discharge of residual waters in Article 121, according to which no one is allowed to discharge into any body or flow of water or on the ground or underground, residual waters that contain pollutants, without prior treatment and the permission or authorization granted by Federal Authority or by the local Authority in the cases of discharges into waters of local jurisdiction or into municipal drainage systems and sewer system of centres of population.

267. Finally, this Law points out that the permission or authorization of discharge of residual waters can be denied or revoked when the Ministry of Environment detects that the residual waters affect or can affect sources of the supply of water (Article 124).

IV. Particular Conditions for Discharge

268. In accordance with section XIV of Article 3 of the Waters Act, particular conditions for discharge are defined as 'the group of physical, chemical, and biological parameters and of their maximum levels allowed in the discharges of residual water, determined by "the Commission" or for the Organization of Basins that corresponds, according to their respective competences, to each user for a certain use or users of a specific receiving body with the purpose of preserving and controlling the quality of the waters according to the present law and the regulations issued under it'.

269. The particular conditions of discharge can be issued for all discharges in the collector nets, rivers, aquifers, basins, beds, glasses, marine waters, and other deposits or in currents of water and the spills of residual waters on the ground or their infiltration into lands (Article 123 of Environmental Act).

V. Standards for Discharge (OMNs)

270. As stated by Article 123 of the Environmental Act, all the discharges in collector nets, rivers, aquifers, basins, beds glasses, marine waters, and other deposits or in currents of water and the spills of residual waters on the ground or their infiltration into lands will satisfy the NOMs issued for such effect.

271. Article 119 of the Environmental Act established that the Ministry of Environment will issue Mexican Official Norms that are required to prevent and to control pollution of the national waters in line with the Waters Act, the Regulations under this Act, and other applicable provisions.

272. On the other hand, the Waters Act states, in section XXXVIII of Article 3, that the OMNs are those set forth by SMARNAT in the terms of the Standardization Act related to conservation, security, and quality in the exploitation, use, enjoyment, and administration of the national waters and of the national property referred to in Article 113 of Waters Act.

273. These norms appear under the nomenclature 'Ministry of the Environment'. Thus far, three have been enacted: ONM-001-Ministry of the Environment-1996, which establishes the maximum permissible limits of pollutants in discharges of residual waters in national waters and national property, published in the *Official Journal of the Federation* on 6 January 1997; ONM-002-Ministry of the Environment-1996, which establishes the maximum permissible limits of contamination in discharges of residual waters to urban or municipal sewer systems, published in the *Official Journal of the Federation* on 3 June 1996; and ONM-ECOL-003-1997, which establishes the maximum permissible limits of pollutants for residual waters that are reused in services, published in the *Official Journal of the Federation* on 21 September 1998.

VI. Duties for Discharge

274. In consonance with Article 276 of the Federal Act of Duties (FAD), those individuals or Corporations that permanently, intermittently, or continuously discharge residual waters in rivers, basins, beds, glasses, marine waters, and other deposits or flows of water, as well as those that discharge residual waters in soils or infiltrate them in lands that are national property or that can contaminate underground water or aquifers, by the terms of this Act, are obliged to pay duties for discharge.

275. Article 278 of FAD states that:

> For the use of property under the public domain of the nation such as receiving bodies for discharges of residual waters, the duty will be assessed according to the volume of discharged water and the pollutants contained therein when the discharge surpass the maximum permissible limits set forth under the particular conditions of discharge or for lack of these, by this Law.

276. That is, the assessment of the duty is determined by two precepts of the FDA. On the one hand, Article 276 establishes the generic obligation of paying the assessment without any condition, while on the other hand, Article 278 states that the assessment is caused only when the maximum permissible limits are surpassed.

277. This idea is confirmed by Articles 278(c) and 282 of the FDA. The first Article points out that 'to calculate the duty to pay for each kind of pollutant that surpasses the maximum permissible limits, the volume of residual waters will be considered', while the second Article exempts from payment those taxpayers whose pollutants do not surpass the maximum permissible limits set forth in the FAD or under the particular conditions of discharge.

278. However, Article 112 of the Waters Act points out that:

> The exploitation, use, or enjoyment of property of the public domain of the Nation such as receiving bodies of discharges of residual waters shall require the payment of the duty established by the FAD. The payment is independent of the fulfillment of provisions established by this Law on prevention and control of the quality of the water, by the Environmental Act; and by the Health Act.

279. In this case, in keeping with the principle of legality of the taxes consecrated by section IV of Article 31 of the Mexican Constitution, the approach that should prevail is the one established by tax law, according to which the duty is paid only when the limits are surpassed.

§3. Local Waters Law

280. As soon as waters are allocated to a State or municipal system of drinkable water or a sewer system, the rule established by Article 45 of Waters Act is applicable, according to which:

> The competence of the municipal authorities, with the participation of the local governments in the terms of this Law, exploitation, includes the use or enjoyment of the national waters that have been allocated to them, including the residual ones, from the point of their extraction or of their delivery on the part of 'the Authority of the Water', until the place of their discharge to receiving bodies that are national property.

281. Thus, local governments are deemed competent to legislate on such waters, that is, to regulate the exploitation, use, and even the preservation of the quality and quantity of the waters that have been allocated to them, and, more concretely, to legislate the cycle that begins at the time when national waters flow into the conduits of drinkable water and until the time when the residual waters flow out of the sewer system to be deposited or to infiltrate national bodies of water or the ground.

282. On the other hand, the Environmental Act holds, in Article 119*bis*, that regarding the prevention and control of water pollution, States and municipalities have authority, in accordance with the distribution of competences established by the Act, over the following:

(1) the control of discharges of residual waters to drainage systems and sewer systems;
(2) the enforcement of OMNs, as well as requiring those who generate discharges to these systems but do not fulfil the OMNs, the installation of treatment systems;
(3) the determination of the amount of the corresponding duties so that the municipality or State can carry out the necessary treatment; and
(4) the upgrading of the registration from the discharges to the drainage systems and sewer systems that administer them to be integrated into the national registration of discharges, which are in the charge of the Secretary.

283. In addition, Article 122 of the Environmental Act establishes that residual waters that are discharged into municipal drainage systems and sewer systems or in the basins, rivers, glasses, and other deposits or flows of water, as well as those that infiltrate the ground through any means, and in general, those that spill out onto the ground, coming from public urban uses and industrial or agricultural uses are required to meet the necessary conditions to prevent the following:

(1) pollution of the receiving bodies;
(2) interferences with the processes of purification of waters; and
(3) dysfunctions, impediments, or alterations in the correct uses or in the operation of the systems and in the hydraulic capacity of the basins, beds, glasses, mantle aquifers, and other deposits of national property, as well as of the sewer systems.

284. Pursuant to Article 120 of the Environmental Act, the following are subject to local regulation:

(1) discharges of industrial origin; those derived from agricultural activities; those coming from the application of pesticides, fertilizers, and toxic substances that are discharged to bodies of water assigned to a State or to a sewer system;
(2) the infiltrations that affect mantle aquifers; and
(3) the dumping of solid residuals coming from the treatment of residual waters into bodies and currents of water.

285. In addition, Article 119*bis* of the Environmental Act establishes the responsibilities that correspond to the governments of the States, the municipalities, and the Federal District regarding the prevention and control of water pollution.

286. States and municipalities have the following responsibilities:

- To control discharges of residual waters to the drainage and sewer systems.
- To require those who generate discharges to these systems and do not satisfy the parameters established by OMNs, to install treatment systems.
- To determine the amount of the corresponding duties so that the municipality or the State can carry out the necessary treatment.

- To upgrade the registrations from the discharges to the drainage nets and sewer systems that they administer to integrate them into the national registers of discharges, which is in the charge of the Secretary.

287. The above-mentioned responsibilities coincide with paragraph 2 of Article 88 of the Waters Act, which points out that 'the control of residual water discharges to municipal drainage systems or sewer systems of population centres corresponds to municipalities, with the cooperation of the States when necessary or when it is established by the laws'.

§4. Protection of Marine Waters

288. Marine waters are protected under the Environmental Act, the Federal Act of the Sea, its Regulations on Marine Waters Pollution, and The Law of Dumping in Mexican Marine Zones.

289. Conforming to Article 130 of the Environmental Act, an authorization granted by the Ministry of the Environment is required to discharge residual waters in marine waters. According to this Provision, in granting the authorization, the Ministry must fulfil the requirements established by the Waters Act, its own Regulations, and the applicable OMNs. In addition, Article 130 of the Environmental Act establishes that, in cases of discharges from mobile sources or fixed platforms in the Territorial Sea and the Exclusive Economic Zone, as well as in cases of discharges from facilities on land to the sea, the Ministry of the Environment shall coordinate with the Ministry of Marine Affairs.

290. The Act of the Sea refers to marine water pollution in three ways:

(1) Article 6 states that national sovereignty is exerted regarding the protection and preservation of marine environments, including prevention of its pollution.
(2) Article 21 states that, in the exercise of powers, rights, jurisdictions, and competences of the Nation into Mexican marine zones, the Environmental Act, the Health Act, and their Regulations, the Waters Act and other laws and regulations, including this Act, its Regulations, and the international treatises to prevent, reduce, and control pollution of marine environments shall be applicable.
(3) Article 46 states that the Nation exerts in an Exclusive Economic Zone located out of the Territorial Sea and adjacent to its jurisdiction regarding protection and preservation of marine environments.

291. Besides, the regulations of the Convention on the Prevention of Marine Pollution by Dumping of Wastes and other matters, points out that no person or Corporation can intentionally dump wastes or other matters into the sea without previous authorization granted by the Ministry of Marine Affairs.

292. The Law of Dumping in Mexican Marine Zones was passed in 2014. In consonance with its Article 1, it has the purpose of controlling and preventing pollution or alteration of the sea by dumping in the Mexican marine areas. In that sense, the Law establishes the terms and conditions in which a dumping can be carried out, noting that in accordance with the Act a permit granted by Ministry of Marine affairs is required.

293. Article 3 the Law of Dumping in Mexican Marine Zones describes the assumptions in which a dumping is considered in the Mexican marine areas:

(A) Any deliberate or accidental disposal, introduction or release in Mexican marine areas of wastes or other matter including non-target ballast water from ships, aircraft, platforms, or other constructions.

(B) The deliberate sinking of ships, aircraft, platforms or other constructions, as well as those derived from it;

(C) The storage of wastes or other matter in the seabed or subsoil thereof from ships, aircraft, platforms, or other constructions.

(D) The abandonment of ships, aircraft, platforms or other constructions, or other objects, including fishing gear, for the sole purpose of deliberately disposing of them.

(E) The discharge of any type of organic matter as attractant of biological species, whose aim is not its fishing.

(F) The placing of materials or objects of any nature, in order to create artificial reefs, piers, breakwaters, or any other structure.

(G) The re-suspension of sediment, consisting of the return of deposited sediment, to a suspended state in the body of water, by any method or procedure, which results in its sedimentation.

294. To define what is to be understood as Mexican marine zones, the Law in question refers to the Federal Law of the Sea, that in its Article 3 indicates that the Mexican marine areas are the following:

A) The Territorial Sea,

B) The Inland Marine Waters,

C) The Contiguous Zone,

D) The Exclusive Economic Zone,

E) The Continental Shelf and the Insular, and

F) Any other permitted by international law.

295. However, the Law of Dumping in Mexican Marine Zones establishes the procedure for obtaining the permit of dumping. Article 18 indicates the required documentation and in Chapter III of the Law, Articles 8–17 establish the evaluation criteria for the authorization of the permit.

296. Finally, the Law states that the Ministry of Marine Affairs is empowered to carry out inspection and monitoring visits on compliance with the Law. In this way, it points out that derived from these activities, the Secretariat may impose preventive measures tending to avoid contamination or alteration of the marine environment or affect to human health. It also indicates a list of infractions, sanctions, which may be imposed by the Secretariat. Article 41 establishes as infringements of the following conduct:

(a) To omit to inform of dumping made by reasons of force majeure.
(b) Failure to fulfil the obligations referred to in Article 27.
(c) Updating any of the cases referred to in Article 54.
(d) The obligations provided for in Article 23 are not fulfilled.
(e) Failure to comply with the Agreements that is pursuant to this Law, issued by the Secretariat.
(f) Failure to comply with the terms specified in the permit of dumping.
(g) To abandon a ship, aircraft, naval device, structure, or platform, without informing the Secretariat in a timely manner.
(h) To carry out verifications without the authorization of the Secretariat.
(i) Perform post-suspension discharges.
(j) Make a discharge after a cancellation.
(k) Incur in any other violation of the provisions of this Law and its Regulations.

297. In regard to sanctions, the Law states in Article 42 the following:

The sanctions will consist of:

I. Suspension of the permit from 1 day to 60 days;

II. Cancellation of the permit, and

III. Fine, which will be determined based on the general minimum wage in force in the Federal District at the time of the violation, from two hundred and fifty to fifty thousand days of minimum wage, depending on the infraction and the damage caused.

The infractions provided for in sections II, V and VI of the previous article shall be sanctioned with suspension of the permit for up to 60 days.

The permit is cancelled, when the permit holder incurs the infractions foreseen in fractions III and IV of the previous article.

The cases provided for in sections I and VII to XI of the preceding article shall be sanctioned with a fine, according to the infraction and the damage caused.

The sanctions mentioned above may be imposed, in more than one of its modalities.

In the event that the period of suspension has expired, without the infractor having remedied the irregularities that gave rise to it, the Secretariat will proceed to the cancellation of the respective permit.

Chapter 4. Wastes

298. In Mexico, the generation, management, and final disposition of wastes are regulated by:

a) The General Act for Prevention and Integral Management of Wastes (hereinafter, the Waste Act),

b) The Regulation under the Waste Act,[36]

c) The Environmental Act,

d) 37 MONs,

e) Local laws, and

f) A number of municipal ordinances related to public service of management of residuals.

299. Local laws and municipal regulations generally govern issues related to domestic wastes and industrial wastes that are not considered dangerous, whereas the Environmental Act establishes few rules about the generation, management, and final disposal of hazardous wastes. However, the most important legal body in regard to waste is the Waste Act.

300. The Waste Act is a comprehensive Act that broadly governs hazardous wastes, industrial wastes, and domestic wastes. This Law defines these three types of waste as follows:

- Hazardous wastes are those presenting some of the following characteristics: corrosiveness, reactivity, explosively, toxicity, flammability, or having infectious agents that confer upon them danger, as well as their containers, recipients, packing, and floors that have been contaminated when they are transferred to another place (Article 5, section XXXII).
- Wastes of special management are those generated in the productive processes that do not gather the characteristics to be considered as dangerous or solid urban residuals, or that are produced by large generators of solid urban residuals (Article 5, section XXX).
- Solid urban wastes are those generated in houses from the elimination of the materials that are used in domestic activities; those from products that have been

36. DOF, 30 Nov. 2006.

consumed and their containers or packing; the residuals that come from any other activity inside establishments or on public roads that generate residuals with characteristic domiciliary; and the resultants of the cleaning of the roads and public places, whenever they are not considered by the Waste Act to be residuals of another nature (Article 5, section XXXIII).

301. In addition, this Act asserts that incompatible wastes are those that in contact or mixed with water or other materials or wastes, react producing heat, pressure, fire, particles, gases, or steams (Article 5, section XXXI).

302. The Waste Act distributes jurisdictions on these issues among the three levels of government, leaving the Federation with the powers related to regulation, standardization, planning, inspection, and surveillance in the dangerous residues.

303. Among the policy instruments for the comprehensive management of hazardous waste, this Law includes:

- The National Program for the Prevention and Integral Management of Waste,
- Management plans,
- Authorizations and permissions,
- Security measures,
- Inspection and surveillance,
- The right to information,
- Social participation,
- The popular complaint.

304. However, although the Waste Act is the specific law of the subject, the Environmental Act retained the regulation of certain aspects, such as the authorization referred to in Article 151*bis* to:

I. The provision of services to third parties for the operation of systems for the collection, storage, transportation, reuse, treatment, recycling, incineration and final disposal of hazardous wastes;

II. The installation and operation of systems for the treatment or final disposal of hazardous waste, or for their recycling when it is intended to recover energy, by incineration, and

III. The installation and operation, by the generator of hazardous waste, of systems for its reuse, recycling and final disposal, outside the facility where the waste was generated.

305. Similarly, Article 153 of the Environmental Act regulates import of hazardous waste, establishing the following rules:

(a) The Ministry of the Environment shall be responsible for the ecological control and surveillance of hazardous materials or wastes imported or to be exported, applying the corresponding security measures, without prejudice to what the Customs Law provides for on this matter.
(b) Import of hazardous materials or waste may only be authorized for its treatment, recycling, or reuse, when its use is in accordance with Mexican laws, OMNs, and other provisions in force.
(c) Import of hazardous materials or wastes whose only object is their final disposal or simple deposit, storage, or confinement in the national territory or in the zones where the nation exercises its sovereignty and jurisdiction, or when its use or manufacture is not allowed in the country in which it has been drawn up.
(d) Transit through the national territory of hazardous materials that do not meet the specifications of use or consumption according to which they were elaborated, or whose elaboration, use, or consumption are prohibited or restricted in the country to which they are destined, cannot be authorized; nor may the transit of such hazardous materials or waste be authorized, when they come from abroad to be destined for a third country.
(e) Granting of authorizations for the export of hazardous materials or waste shall be subject to the express consent of the recipient country.
(f) Hazardous materials and waste generated in the production, processing, processing or repair processes in which raw material introduced into the country under the temporary importation regime, including those regulated in Article 85 of the Customs Law, have to be returned to the country of origin within the period determined by the Ministry for such effect.

306. Granting of authorizations by the Ministry for the importation or exportation of hazardous materials or waste shall be subject to duly ensuring compliance with the provisions of this Law and other applicable provisions, as well as the redress of damages That could be caused both in the national territory and abroad; likewise, the export of hazardous waste must be refused when re-importation into the national territory is contemplated: there is no express consent of the recipient country; the country of destination requires reciprocity; or implies a breach of the commitments assumed by Mexico in the International Treaties and Conventions in the matter.In addition to other applicable provisions, the authorizations granted for the import or export of hazardous materials and waste may be revoked, without prejudice to the imposition of the corresponding sanctions, in the following cases:

(a) when by supervening causes, it is found that the authorized hazardous materials or waste pose a greater risk to the ecological balance than that considered for the granting of the corresponding authorization;
(b) when the import or export operation does not comply with the requirements established in the ecological guide issued by the Secretariat;
(c) when the hazardous materials or waste no longer have the attributes or characteristics according to which they were authorized; and

307. When it is determined that the authorization was transferred to a person other than the one that requested the authorization, or when the corresponding request contains false information, or presented in a way that conceals information necessary for the correct assessment of the request.

308. The LGEEPA also refers to the reuse and recycling of hazardous waste, pointing out in Article 152:

> The Secretariat will promote programs to prevent and reduce the generation of hazardous wastes, as well as to encourage their reuse and recycling.
>
> In those cases where hazardous waste can be used in a process other than the one that generated them, the Regulations of this Law and the Mexican official standards that are issued, shall establish the mechanisms and procedures that make possible their efficient management from the point Environmental and economic view.
>
> Hazardous waste that is used, treated or recycled in a process other than the one that generated them, within the same site, will be subject to internal control by the responsible company, in accordance with the formalities established in the Regulations of this Law.
>
> In the event that the waste indicated in the previous paragraph is transported to a site other than that in which it is generated.

309. Finally, the Environmental Act also refers in Articles 151 and 152*bis* to the subject of responsibility for the management of hazardous waste.

310. As mentioned above, the Waste Act regulates these four types of residuals, but in Article 9, section II, it allows the States to enact their own local laws so as to enforce the Waste Act according to their particular circumstances; and, in Article 95, holds that 'the regulation of the generation and integral management of solid urban residuals and the residuals of special management shall be carried out, according to established Law, by the applicable dispositions enacted by the local congresses and other legal provisions'.

311. Article 7 of the Waste Act states that the Federal government's regulatory and normative responsibilities regarding hazardous waste include the following:

(a) To issue regulations, Mexican norms, and other official legal provisions to regulate the integral management of the dangerous residuals and their classification, and to prevent the contamination of places or to carry out their restoration when it happens (section II).

(b) To issue regulations, Mexican norms, and other official legal provisions to regulate the integral management of the residuals of the metallurgic mining industry that correspond to their conformity with this Law and the Mining Law (section III).

(c) To issue OMNs for the integral management of solid urban waste and of wastes of special management (section IV).

(d) To issue OMNs for establishing the approaches to determine what residuals will be subject to management plans that include the listings of these, and that they specify the procedures to be continued in the establishment of these plans (section V).

(e) To issue OMNs establishing, among others, environmental and technological efficiency criteria to be met by materials used to elaborate products, containers, packaging and plastic packaging, and discarded Styrofoam that become waste. Such standards must consider the principles of reduce, recycle, and reuse in handling them (section VI).

(f) To regulate and to control hazardous wastes coming from small generators, large generators, or micro-generators, when these last are not controlled by local governments (section VII).

(g) To regulate the environmental aspects related to the transport of hazardous wastes (section VIII).

(h) To enact the official Mexican norms to prevent pollution for residuals whose final disposition can provoke salinization and excessive increments of organic loads on the ground and in bodies of water (section XXVII).

§1. Hazardous Wastes

312. Hazardous wastes are regulated by both the Environmental Act and the Waste Act.

The Environmental Act refers to this regulatory activity from three perspectives:

- Articles 150, 151, and 151*bis* focus on regulating the generation and final disposition of hazardous wastes.
- Articles 28 and 30 condition the generation, management, and final disposition of hazardous wastes upon the previous granting of an authorization of the EIA and the presentation of a study of risk.
- Articles 5, 7, 8, and 9 establish the rules related to the system of shared competences among the federation, States, and municipalities regarding hazardous wastes. Pursuant to such provisions, the regulation and control of the operation of sites for final disposition of hazardous wastes are exclusively the responsibility of the Federal Authorities.

313. In line with Article 150 of the Environmental Act, hazardous wastes should be managed in accordance with:

- the Environmental Act,
- the Regulations under the Environmental Act regarding hazardous wastes, and
- MONs issued on this matter.

314. However, it is important to mention that the Environmental Act only refers to four aspects related to hazardous wastes, which were developed by the Regulations and the MONs, as will be explained further on. These aspects are the following:

(1) authorization to operate gathering systems, storage, transport, reuse, treatment, recycling, incineration, and final disposition of hazardous wastes (Article 151*bis* to, sections I and II);
(2) reuse and recycling of hazardous wastes (Articles 151*bis* III and 152);
(3) import, export, and traffic in national territory of wastes and materials (Article 153);
(4) liability for the generation, management, and final disposition of hazardous wastes and materials (Articles 151 and 152*bis*).

315. Article 151*bis* of the Environmental Act, section I, points out that 'providing services of operation of systems for the gathering, storage, transport, reuse, treatment, recycling, incineration, and final disposition of hazardous waste' requires previous authorization from the Secretary.

316. Additionally, in Article 150, the Environmental Act points out that Regulations regarding hazardous wastes as well as the OMNs shall contain the approaches and listings that identify and classify the materials and hazardous wastes based on their level of danger and their characteristics and volumes.

317. The Environmental Act establishes two authorizations as mechanisms to control those who lend the reception and final disposition of hazardous waste service: an environmental impact authorization and an authorization that expressly is required to lend these services. Both authorizations are the exclusive responsibility of the Federal Authorities.

318. In addition, the generation, management, and final disposition of hazardous wastes are also regulated by the Waste Act. This Act points out in Article 1, section V that its objectives are, among others, 'to regulate the generation and integral management of dangerous wastes', which is the reason why it dedicates specific titles to regulate the integral management of hazardous wastes (Articles 40–94).

319. The Waste Act focuses more on the requirements that those interested in building and operating hazardous waste disposal sites must fulfil. Article 65 of this Law states that:

> The facilities for the final disposal of hazardous wastes shall have the necessary characteristics to prevent and to reduce the possible migration of the residuals outside of the cells, in accordance with what establishes the Regulations and the applicable MONs.

320. In this regard, the Regulation under the Waste Act sets up in its Article 92 the criteria that must be observed in selecting the site, designing, building, and operating of cells for landfills. Such criteria are:

> I. Geological, geophysical, hydrological and hydrogeological characteristics of the site;

II. Type, quantity and characteristics of the waste to be confined;

III. Lixiviation that produce hazardous waste to be confined;

IV. Potential migration of contaminants in soil; and

V. Impact and vulnerability associated with the activity.

321. There have been issued two ONMS in regard to hazardous waste disposal facilities. The first of them is the ONM-057-Ministry of the Environment-1993, which, in item 1.5, refers to the design and construction of final disposal cells. The OMN establishes nine requirements for the construction of the disposal cells, which have to be properly fulfilled for the project's approval and the evaluation of its environmental impact. On the other hand, the OMN establishes six restrictions for the construction of cells, which have to be taken into account during the evaluation of the environmental impact.

322. The second OMN is the OMN-055-SEMARNAT-2003 that establishes the requirements to be met by site designated to controlled confining of hazardous waste previously stabilized.

323. Regarding the location of sites for the final disposition of hazardous wastes, the Waste Act requires that they be kept the minimum distance from population centres larger than 1,000 inhabitants. Indeed, paragraph 2 of Article 65 of the Act holds that:

> The minimum distance that facilities for disposal of hazardous wastes must be kept from population centres larger than one thousand inhabitants, according to the last population census, shall not be less than 5 kilometres, and, when their location is planned, it shall be necessary to take into consideration the ecological classification of the territory and the applicable urban development plans.

324. The Waste Act also established mechanisms for the management and final disposition of hazardous wastes several authorizations. In this regard, Article 50 requires that authorization be granted by the Ministry of the Environment for the following:

(a) the management of hazardous wastes;
(b) the use of hazardous wastes in production processes;
(c) the gathering and storage of hazardous wastes generated by third parties;
(d) any activity connected with the management of hazardous waste generated by third parties;
(e) the incineration of hazardous wastes;
(f) the transport of hazardous wastes;
(g) the merging of disposal sites into facilities where hazardous wastes are managed;
(h) the use of thermal treatments of waste by sterilization of termolisis;
(i) the import and export of hazardous wastes.

325. The Waste Act also establishes the obligation of having a Management Plan. The management plan is defined by section XXI of Article 5 of the Waste Act as an instrument to minimize the generation of waste and maximize its value through actions, procedures, and viable means of producers, importers, exporters, distributors, traders, consumers, users of sub-products, and large generators of waste as well as of the three levels of government. These actions must be guided by criteria of environmental, technological, economic, and social efficiency, and by the principles of shared responsibility and integral management of waste.

326. According to Article 31 of Waste Act, generators of the following waste are required to have a management plan:

I. Used lubricating oils;

II. Organic solvents used;

III. Catalytic converters of motor vehicles;

IV. Accumulators of motor vehicles containing lead;

V. Mercury or nickel-cadmium batteries;

VI. Fluorescent and mercury vapor lamps;

VII. Additions containing mercury, cadmium or lead;

VIII. Drugs;

IX. Pesticides and their packaging containing remnants thereof;

X. Persistent organic compounds such as polychlorinated biphenyls;

XI. Oil-based drilling muds from the extraction of fossil fuels and sludge from wastewater treatment plants when considered hazardous;

XII. Blood and its components, only in their liquid form, as well as their derivatives;

XIII. The strains and cultures of pathogens generated in the diagnostic and research procedures and in the production and control of biological agents;

XIV. Pathological residues consisting of tissues, organs and parts that are removed during necropsies, surgery or any other type of surgery that is not contained in formaldehyde, and

XV. Puncture-staining residues that have been in contact with humans or animals or their biological samples during diagnosis and treatment, including scalpel blades, lancets, integrated needle syringes, hypodermic needles, acupuncture needles and tattoos.

327. In the same vein, the following are obliged to prepare a management plan:

- Whoever uses, produces, sells, or disposes of used, out-of-date, recalled, or disposed of products that are classified as such the Mexican Official Standard NOM-161-SEMARNAT-2014.
- Large generators of hazardous waste, who additionally must submit to the consideration of SEMARNAT said management plan and submit an annual report on the generation and management of their hazardous waste.
- Small generators of hazardous waste, who must subject their waste to management plans, although they do not necessarily have to obtain approval from SEMARNAT.
- Micro-generators of hazardous waste, who must submit to management plans and conditions established by local government authorities, i.e., management plans should not be approved by SEMARNAT, but by local authorities, since, as it has been pointed out previously, the regulation of micro-generators, by virtue of the agreements signed between SEMARNAT and local governments, has been left to the authorities of each local state.

328. Although there is clearly established the obligation to have a management plan, not all generators of hazardous waste have them and still less, have obtained approval or approval from the corresponding authority.

329. This is perhaps because there are no specific guidelines that define the content of these management plans.

330. Article 17 of the Regulations of the LGPGIR states that management plans must be formulated in accordance with the LGPGIR and its Regulations, the corresponding Mexican official standards but even though in 2011 the Draft Official Standard Mexican company PORY-NOM-160-SEMARNAT -2011, almost four years have passed and the standard has not yet been published, so the guidelines for the uniform preparation of hazardous waste management plans are not clear.

331. Finally, the Waste Act considers few authorizations in the field.

332. These authorizations are linked to management activities and not to the generation of hazardous waste. Regarding the generation of hazardous waste, the only obligation that is established is to register with the Ministry of the Environment in the case of large generators or whit the local authorities, in the case of small generators.

333. According to 50 of the Waste Act conducting the following activities related to the management of hazardous waste need authorization from the Ministry of Environment:

I. Provision of hazardous waste management services;

II. The use of hazardous waste in productive processes;

III. The collection and storage of hazardous waste from third parties;

IV. The performance of any of the activities related to the handling of hazardous waste from third parties;

V. The incineration of hazardous waste;

VI. Transportation of hazardous waste;

VII. Establishment of containments within facilities where hazardous waste is handled;

VIII. The transfer of authorizations issued by the Secretariat;

IX. The use of thermal treatments of residues by sterilization or thermolysis;

X. The import and export of hazardous waste, and

XI. The others that establish by Mexican Laws.

334. The procedure for obtaining the aforementioned authorizations is defined in Chapter III of Title Four of the Regulation under Waste Act entitled 'Hazardous Wastes', and only makes exceptions regarding the procedure for the import and export of hazardous wastes that are regulated in a different Title.

335. In this case, what is to be done is to submit the application in the format established by the Ministry of Environment, clearly indicate the activity or activities in respect of which the authorization is requested, pay the corresponding rights, present the applicant's identification or the constitutive act which indicates in the corporate purpose that the company can carry out the activity for which authorization is requested as legal administrative documents.

336. It must also present a land use authorization issued by the corresponding authority that allows it to operate said activity in the requested terms, a plan of the executive project, the flow diagram of the process, and, where appropriate, the authorization of Federal environmental impact. All these as technical data.

337. Finally, they must have a staff-training programme and a programme for the prevention and care of contingencies or environmental emergencies and accidents.

338. In this case, obtaining an authorization depends on the accreditation of the requested requirements, above all, that the technical capacity is demonstrated and that the permits associated with such activity, such as land use and environmental impact, are available.

339. The authorizations issued may be extended whenever requested with forty-five days prior to the expiration of the validity, that the activity developed is the same as that authorized, that the hazardous wastes that were authorized continue to be handled and that the person requesting it is the holder of the authorization that is intended to be extended.

§2. Waste of Special Management and Urban Solid Waste

340. In accordance with section II of Article 10 of the Waste Act the municipalities are responsible for the integral management of urban solid waste that consists of the gathering, transference, treatment, and final disposition, according to the following responsibilities: to enact regulations and other juridical or administrative dispositions of general observance inside their respective jurisdictions so as to enforce the present Law and the legal dispositions enacted by the states.

341. The Waste Act refers only to wastes requiring special management and to urban solid waste in Articles 95–100. In this regard, the Waste Act basically establishes matters on which local and municipal governments can legislate.

342. Regarding incompatible waste, the Waste Act just refers to prohibiting their confining in the same place or cell (Article 67, section VI) and to establish sanctions for mixing incompatible waste (Article 106, section III).

Chapter 5. Soil Pollution

343. Soil pollution is an inappropriately ruled by the current environmental legislation because it is associated almost exclusively with the disposal of waste even when it results from various causes.

344. The Environmental Law contains a chapter called 'prevention and control of soil pollution' which is composed of Articles 134–144. Almost all these legal precepts are programmatic and only, Article 137 states that it is subject to the authorization by municipalities or by the Federal District, the operation of the collection, storage, transportation, accommodation, reuse, treatment, and final disposal of municipal solid waste systems.

345. In the same vein, Article 142 prohibits import of waste for its spillage, deposit, confinement, storage, incineration, or any treatment for its destruction in the national territory or in the areas in which the nation exercises sovereignty or jurisdiction. However, these two precepts only refer to soil pollution indirectly.

346. Finally, according to Article 141 of the Environmental Act, the Ministry of Environment, in coordination with the Ministries of Economy and Health, shall issue the OMNs for manufacture and use of containers and packages for all kinds of products whose materials make possible the reduction of solid waste generation.

347. The rest of the provisions of this chapter are much more programmatic and refer to the criteria for the prevention and control of soil contamination, the issuance of OMNs in this area and the process of getting into coordination agreements with the states and the municipalities.

348. By contrasts, in a different chapter, Article 152*bis* specifically refers to soil pollution and establishes a parameter of soil remediation stating:

> When the generation, management or final disposal of hazardous materials and waste produces soil pollution, those responsible for these operations must carry out the necessary actions to recover and restore the conditions of the soil, so that it can be destined to any of the activities foreseen in the urban development program or of ecological ordinance plan that results applicable for the specific site or area.

349. The Waste Act also contains a chapter on soil pollution called 'liability for contamination and remediation of sites', which includes Articles 68–79.

350. The chapter governs fundamentally five issues: the obligation to repair the damages caused by soil contamination; authorization for the transfer of contaminated sites; abandonment of contaminated sites; identification, inventory, registration, and categorization of sites contaminated with hazardous wastes; and remediation declarations.

351. Transfer of polluted sites is in principle banned by Article 71 of the Waste Law, but this prohibition can be lifted by means of the authorization granted by the Ministry of Environment.

352. In the case of sites contaminated by hazardous waste that are abandoned, Article 73 of the Waste Law provides that the Ministry of Environment, in coordination with state and municipal governments, may formulate and execute the corresponding remediation programmes and make effective the guarantees provided by those who abandoned the site in question.

Likewise, under Article 75 of the Waste Act, the Ministry of the Environment and local governments are obliged to carry out actions of identification, inventory, registration, and categorization of sites contaminated with hazardous waste, to proceed to its remediation.

353. Finally, according to Article 74 of the Waste Law, the Remediation Declarations may establish modalities to the property right, but the Law does not indicate to whom it corresponds to issue such declarations.

Chapter 6. Noise and Vibrations

354. The issue addressed in this chapter is one of the least treated by Mexican environmental legislation and because of this also by jurisprudence.

355. First, the LGEEPA refers to all these issues from the perspective of jurisdictions between the three levels of government. Article 5, section XV, empowers the federal government to regulate prevention of environmental pollution caused by noise, vibrations, thermal energy, light, electromagnetic radiation, and odours that could result harmful to the ecological balance and the environment; while in accordance with Article 7, section VII, states have the power to prevent and control pollution generated by such pollutants when they come from fixed and mobile sources that are not of federal jurisdiction. Finally, in accordance with Article 8, section VI, municipalities are responsible for enforcing regulations on these matters in the case of commercial facilities and services.

356. On the other hand, Title Four of the Environmental Act contains a chapter VIII called 'Noise, Vibrations, Thermal and Luminous Energy, Smells and Visual Pollution.' This chapter is integrated by only two precepts that seek to lay the groundwork for regulation of all forms of pollution to which the nomenclature of the chapter refers and obviously, it is an incomplete regulation.

357. The regulatory content of Article 155 may be summarized as follows:

(A) Prohibits the emission of noise, vibrations, thermal and light energy and generation of visual pollution, as soon as they exceed the maximum limits established in OMNs issue by the Ministry of environment.

(B) The federal or local authorities, according to their field of competence, will take the measures to prevent that these limits are transgressed and, if applicable, apply the corresponding sanctions.

(D) In the construction of works or installations that generate thermal or light energy, noise or vibrations, as well as in the operation or operation of existing ones, preventive and corrective actions must be taken to avoid the harmful effects of such contaminants on the ecological balance and the atmosphere.

358. On the other hand, Article 156 of the Environmental Law states the following rules:

A) Official Mexican standards on noise, vibration, thermal and light energy and the generation of visual pollution shall establish procedures to prevent and control pollution from these causes and shall set up the respective emission limits.

B) The Ministry of Health will carry out the necessary analyses, studies, investigations and surveillance to determine the origin or origin, nature, degree, magnitude and frequency of the emissions to determine when health damages occur.

C) The Ministry of the Environment, in coordination with public or private, national or international organizations, will integrate the information related to this type of pollution, as well as methods and technology to control and treat it.

359. Law, those who emit smells, gases or solid or liquid particles into the atmosphere, should include them in the processing and obtaining of the licence of operation or unique environmental licence which we have already analysed in the part corresponding to the air pollution, since this precept indicates:

> ARTICLE 111 BIS.- For the operation and operation of fixed sources of federal jurisdiction that emit or can emit smells, gases or solid or liquid particles into the atmosphere, authorization from the Secretariat will be required.

360. By 2008, just four OMNs regulating noise pollution had been published by the SEMARNAT (OMN-079-SEMARNAT-1994, establishing the maximum permissible limits of noise emissions from new vehicles in factories and their method of measurement; OMN-080-SEMARNAT-1994, establishing the maximum permissible limits of emissions of noise from automobiles and motorcycles on the road; OMN-081-SEMARNAT-1994, establishing the maximum permissible limits of noise from fixed sources and their method of measurement; and OMN-082- SEMARNAT-1994, establishing the maximum permissible limits of noise emissions from new motorcycles in factories and their method of measurement).

361. In addition, a OMN the NOM-036-SCT3-2000, that establishes the maximum permissible limits of noise emission by subsonic jet aircraft, propeller-driven, supersonic and helicopters, its measurement method, and the requirements to comply with these limits whereas no NOM on vibrations has been passed yet.

362. It is important to mention that in 1982, a regulation under the Federal Act for Environmental Protection on Pollution from Noise Emissions was issued by the Executive. That Regulation is still in force when it does not contradict the Environmental Act. According to the Regulation, the maximum level of noise emissions from fixed sources is 68 decibels from six to twenty-two hours and 65 decibels from twenty-two to six hours (Article 11). In cases of mobile sources, the Regulation establishes that the maximum level of emissions is from 79 to 84 decibels (Article 29).

Part II. Nature Conservation and Management

363. Mexican law and policy regarding nature conservation and management is based on the rules established by the Federal Constitution in relation to: (a) the power of the Nation to impose limitations and modalities on private property of lands and waters, (b) the power of the Nation to regulate the use and exploitation of natural resources, and (c) the concurrent jurisdictions system to legislate on environmental issues.

364. In accordance with the concurrent legislative system introduced by Article 73, paragraph XXIX(g) of the Federal Constitution, Mexican biodiversity protection policy is based on the rules established by the Environmental Act, the Wildlife Conservation Act, and the General Act for Sustainable Forest Development as well as on the provisions contained into local laws passed by local congresses in these matters. These laws refer to a series of mechanisms directed toward the protection of natural resources, as explained below.

Chapter 1. Protected Natural Areas

365. In 1922, the Isla de Guadalupe was established as the first natural reserve in Mexico, and in 1935, the volcanoes Iztacihuatl and Popocatepetl were declared the first national parks. However, the national protected natural-areas system as a mechanism of protecting habitats and natural resources was incorporated into Mexican environmental law until 1988, when the Environmental Act was passed.

366. Currently, 176 protected natural areas have been established, comprising 12.92% of the national territory.[37]

367. The Environmental Law refers to protected natural areas (PNAs) in First Chapter of the Second Title called 'Biodiversity'. The mentioned chapter I is integrated by Articles 44–77*bis* and has been regulated by the Regulation of the General Law of the Ecological Equilibrium and the Protection to the Environment on Protected Natural Areas.

368. The Environmental Act defines a natural protected natural area as 'a region in the national territory where the environment has not been notably affected by human activity or needs to be preserved and restored' (Article 3, section II and Article 44). However, this definition should be complemented by the provisions of the second paragraph of Article 44 and Article 57 of the mentioned Law. The first of them, modified in 1996, states that 'Owners, possessors or holders of other rights over lands, waters and forests included within protected natural areas shall be subject to the modalities that, in accordance with this Law, and the other provisions contained in the management program and in the corresponding ecological planning programs', while the second states that protected natural areas are established by Executive Order, issued by the federal or local government.

369. In this way it can be concluded that the declarations of PNAs are acts of the Executive that impose 'Modalities or limitations' on the property rights of the lands that these comprise with the object of preserving or restoring the environments present in them.

370. Pursuant to Article 46 of the LGEEPA, there are the following categories of PNAs:

A) Reserves of the biosphere.

B) National parks.

C) Natural monuments.

D) Areas of protection of natural resources.

37. . *See* : http://www.conanp.gob.mx/.

E) Areas of protection of flora and fauna.

F) Sanctuaries.

G) State Parks and Reserves, as well as other categories established by local legislation.

H) Municipal ecological conservation zones, as well as other categories established by local legislation.

I) Areas Voluntarily intended for conservation.

371. Each one of the above categories differs from the other by the characteristics of the environments present as the modalities imposed by the corresponding declaration.

372. The PNAs establish the different uses that can be given to the soil on which they are established. The original text of the Environmental Act of 1988 indicated that in the case of biosphere reserves the limitations to the right of property that were established in the respective Declaration Decree should be different for the core area than for the buffer zone of the PNAs.

373. Land use restrictions in the core area should be greater because in that area is the natural phenomenon that is intended to protect, while in the buffer zone could withstand greater uses because it is an area that protects the core area of the external impact. However, a later reform also established for the rest of the PNAs different zone divisions with diverse use soil restrictions.

374. Given the system of concurrent jurisdiction that governs environmental matters under Article 73, section XXIX-G of the Constitution, PNAs can be established by both the federal government and local governments. According to Article 46 of the Environmental Act, the federal government has the power to declare six different categories of PNAs: biosphere reserves, national parks, natural monuments, areas for protection of natural resources, areas for protection of flora and fauna, and sanctuaries; while local governments (states and Federal District) have the power to establish state parks and reserves and other categories established by state legislation and to municipalities it corresponds to establish municipal ecological conservation zones, as well as other categories, according to local legislation.

375. Declarations of PNAs do not expropriate land ownership but deprive the owner of a series of prerogatives inherent in the right of property.

In this regard, Article 63 of the Environmental Law states that:

> 'The protected natural areas established by the Federal Executive may include, partially or totally, properties subject to any property regime', but the second paragraph of article 44 states that 'Owners, possessors or Holders of other rights over land, water and forests included within natural protected areas shall be

> subject to the modalities that, in accordance with this Law, establish the decrees establishing such areas, as well as the other provisions contained in the program Management systems and in the corresponding ecological management programs.'

On the other hand, in principle, land owners where NPAs are decreed lose the right to administer this. This is clear from the reading of Article 47 of the LGEEPA which states:

> In the establishment, administration and management of the protected natural areas referred to in the preceding article, the Ministry (of the Environment) shall promote the participation of its inhabitants, owners or holders, local governments, indigenous peoples, and other public and private social organizations with the aim of promoting the integral development of the community and ensuring the protection and preservation of ecosystems and their biodiversity.

376. For this purpose, the Ministry of the Environment may sign with the interested parties the coordination and cooperation agreements that correspond.

377. Similarly, the second paragraph of Article 65 states that: 'Once a protected natural area of federal competence has been established, the Secretariat shall designate the Director of the area concerned who shall be responsible for coordinating the formulation, implementation, and evaluation of the corresponding management program, in accordance with the provisions of this Law and the provisions deriving therefrom.'

Chapter 2. Wildlife Protection

378. Although in Mexico the flora and fauna were subject of legal protection from long time ago[38] - The laws of hunting and fishing regulated the exploitation of wildlife in our country since before the Stockholm Summit in 1972[39] - The comprehensive protection of biodiversity is not yet a reality.

379. The original text of the Environmental Act of 1988 already included in its Title III to the rational use of natural elements.

380. However, since the 1990s, under the influence of the Convention on Biological Diversity (CBD), the paradigm of protection of the natural resources of wild and aquatic flora and fauna and of their habitat acquires a different dimension. In almost all the jurisdictions the isolated consideration of these elements is substituted by its integral regulation.

381. The CBD transforms the paradigm of the protection of what until then we denominated natural resources, because this International Treaty constructs all its normative structure based on a new legal category, that is to say: the biodiversity. This normative category is defined by the CBD as the variability of life, including terrestrial and aquatic ecosystems, the ecological complexes of which they form part, the diversity within each species and between species (Article 2 of the CBD).

382. The Environmental Act of 1988 did not regulate all the aspects contemplated in the CBD, so in 2000 the Law on Wildlife was approved, in 2003 the General Law of Sustainable Forest Utilization was passed, in 2007 the General Law of Fishing and Aquaculture Sustainable came into force, and in 2012 the General Law of Climate Change was passed as well. All these laws deal with various aspects relating to the protection of biodiversity. However, the new legislative framework that is constructed with all these laws is far from being consistent and comprehensive.

383. Protection: These include a number of commitments to protect wildlife and their habitats, such as the Convention Concerning Wetlands of International Importance Especially as Waterfowl Habitat (Ramsar Convention); The Convention for the Protection of the World Cultural and Natural Heritage (Paris Convention); The Convention on International Trade in Endangered Species of Wild Fauna and Flora (CITES); Convention between the United Mexican States and the United States of America for the Protection of Migratory Birds and Hunting Mammals; and The United Nations Convention on the Law of the Sea (Montego Bay Convention).

384. Based on the third paragraph of Article 27 of the CPEUM as well as on the principles established by the international treaties signed by Mexico environmental

38. The Hunting Act of 1952 and 1940, Mexican Fisheries Act of 1950, Fisheries Act of 1947, Mexican Pacific Watershed Law of the Pacific Ocean and Gulf of California of 1938, Fisheries Act of 1932, Of Maritime and River Fisheries of the Mexican Republic of 1926, and Fisheries Act of 1925.
39. The Stockholm Summit refers to the Conference held in this city on 16 Jun. 1972, attended by 110 countries and for the first time the International Community discussed the issue of the Environment. The outcome of this Conference was the Stockholm Declaration on the Human Environment with twenty-six principles to follow.

legislation establishes several mechanisms aimed at regulating the use of flora and fauna resources that are susceptible to appropriation.

385. Nowadays, in Mexico there is a complex but incomplete environmental framework that deals in an unsystematic way with biodiversity protection. This system is based on the establishment of a series of permits, licences, and authorizations, taxes with extra-fiscal purposes and modalities to the right of ownership.

386. The Environmental Law states in its Article 82 that: 'The provisions of this Law are applicable to the possession, administration, preservation, repopulation, propagation, import, export and development of wild flora and fauna and genetic material, without prejudice of what anothers legal bodies establish', however, this law only regulates in a non-systematic way some of the aspects related to this subject.

387. Indeed, the Second Title of the Environmental Law refers to the protection of biodiversity in different ways. Thus, Chapter I of this Title is dedicated to the protection of the habitat of biodiversity through the national system of protected natural areas. The second chapter of the same title deals with the restoration of habitats altered or in the process of alteration by desertification or degradation. Finally, the third chapter of the title that we analyse refers specifically to the flora and the fauna.

388. On the other hand, Title Three of the Environmental Law refers to the sustainable use of natural elements but excluding aquatic ecosystems.

389. Natural protected areas have already been analysed in another section of this book and aspects related to restoration will be analysed in the last part of this book so in this section we will only refer to the third of Title Two of the Environmental Law.

390. Articles 79–87*bis* 2 of the Environmental Law establish very basic instruments for the protection of flora and fauna that in no way exhaust the series of aspects that Article 82, previously transcribed, announces as the material scope of application of the same. Thus, Article 79 establishes ten criteria to which the preservation and exploitation of wild flora and fauna must be subject, while Article 80 states that these criteria must be considered during the exercise of various acts of authority relating to the protection of flora and fauna.

391. However, other precepts of the mentioned chapter establish criteria additional to those mentioned by Article 79 that govern the issuance of specific acts of authority, such as:

(a) The use of natural resources in areas that are the habitat of wild flora and fauna, especially endemic, threatened, or endangered species must be done in a way that does not alter the necessary conditions for subsistence, development, and evolution of these species (Article 83).
(b) The exploitation of species of wild flora and fauna in economic activities may be authorized when individuals guarantee their controlled reproduction or development in captivity or semi-weeds or when the exploitation rate is lower than that of natural renewal of populations, in accordance with Mexican official Norms issued by the Secretariat (Article 87).
(c) The exploitation of threatened or endangered species may not be permitted except in cases where their controlled reproduction and the development of populations of the corresponding species are guaranteed (Article 87, second paragraph).

(d) Authorization for the sustainable use of endemic species shall be granted in accordance with OMNs issued by the Ministry of Environment, only if such use does not threaten or endanger the species (Article 87, third paragraph)

392. Other precepts of the chapter that we are analysing grant to the Ministry of Environment a series of faculties in the matter, for instance: to establish, to modify, and to close banned seasons of flora and fauna (Article 81); issuing OMNs for preservation and sustainable use of wild flora and fauna and other biological resources (Article 84); issuing Mexican official standards to which the use of non-timber forest resources and firewood for domestic uses will be subject to OMNs issued by the Ministry and other applicable provisions; to promote before the Ministry of Economy the establishment of measures of regulation or restriction, totally or partially, to the export or import of specimens of native or exotic wild flora and fauna and impose the necessary restrictions for the circulation or transit through the territory National of species of wild flora and fauna from and destined for the foreigner (Article 85); to apply the provisions on the preservation and sustainable use of wildlife species and other laws and authorize their use in economic activities, without prejudice to the powers of other agencies, according to other laws (Article 85); to authorize the use of species of wild flora and fauna, as well as other biological resources for use in biotechnology; and authorize the collection of species of wild flora and fauna, as well as other biological resources for scientific research purposes (Article 87, fifth paragraph).

393. Finally, the Environmental Law recognizes that although using of flora and fauna requires the authorization from the Ministry of the Environment it also requires the consent of the owners of the land where these resources are located, which is consistent with the provisions of the General Law of Wildlife in the sense that the owners of the land where the wildlife is distributed have a preferential right of use. Thus, Article 87, fourth paragraph, states that 'the exploitation of species of wild flora and fauna requires the express consent of the owner or legitimate possessor of the property in which they are found'. Similarly, Article 87*bis* states that using of wild flora and fauna, as well as other biological resources for use in biotechnology, may only be granted if there is prior, express and informed consent of the owner or legitimate holder of the property in which the biological resource is found.

394. On the other hand, although this chapter does not deal with the establishment of any tax instrument aimed at the protection of wild flora and fauna, it grants to the resources that are obtained from the collection of those taxes that are established in the corresponding legislation, a specific destination. Thus, Article 87*bis* 1 states that the income received by the Federation for the granting of permits, authorizations, and licences in the field of wild flora and fauna, as determined by applicable law, will be used to carry out actions of preservation and restoration of biodiversity in areas that constitute the habitat of wild flora and fauna species for which permits, licences, or authorizations were granted.

395. As we can see, on the one hand, the precepts that make up this chapter of the Environmental Act do not exhaust the catalogue of topics that according to Article 82 should regulate, on the other hand also cover that area of application since Article 87 *bis* 2 refers to the power of the Federal, State, Federal District, and Municipal

Governments, within the scope of their respective competencies, to regulate the dignified and respectful treatment that must be given to animals.

396. The same provision states that it is the responsibility of the federal government to issue Mexican Official Norms that determine the basic principles of dignified and respectful treatment provided by the Environmental Law, which include conditions of captivity, exhibition, transportation, food, exploitation, training, maintenance, and slaughter of animals, as well as monitor their compliance.

397. The General Act of Wildlife (Wildlife Act) was passed in 2000 and gave local governments, the individual States, and the national government shared power to design, implement, and coordinate the policies regarding conservation and sustainable use of wildlife resources. In this Act, provisions related to wildlife apply to wildlife habitats as well (Article 1).

398. Although the Act defines wildlife as 'the organisms that freely subsist in their habitat subject to the processes of natural evolution' (Article 3 section XLVI), its provisions do not apply either to forests or to species that partially or entirely live in water. The Act does not establish who owns the natural resources in Mexico, but it states that 'owners and legal possessors of land, where wildlife exists, have the right to reasonably utilize these resources, as well as to transmit this right to third parties' (Article 4).

399. This Act establishes a series of mechanisms for the protection of nature, such as: (a) a national system of management units for wildlife conservation, (b) legal origin certification, (c) declarations of areas for the protection of wildlife aquatic species, (d) banned seasons, (e) critical habitats, and (f) a licensing and permits procedure.

§1. National System for Managing Wildlife Conservation Units

400. The Wildlife Act created the concept of 'units of management for the conservation of wildlife', which are defined by the Act as those pieces of land and facilities that operate in accordance with an approved management plan, and where the conditions of the habitat and the distribution of the wildlife living there are permanently monitored (Article 3, section XLV).

401. According to Article 39 of the Wildlife Act, landowners or possessors of pieces of land where wildlife is placed are obliged to inform the Ministry of the Environment about these circumstances so that these pieces of land are registered and included, as units for wildlife conservation, in the National System for Wildlife Management.

402. Being the basic elements by which to integrate the National System for Wildlife Management, units of management for the conservation of wildlife have the objective of preserving natural habitats, populations, and specimens of wildlife. Additionally, these units could have specific objectives for restoration, protection, maintenance, recovery, reproduction, repopulation, reintroduction, rescue, rehabilitation, exhibition, recreation, environmental education, and sustainable exploitation.

403. The Wildlife Act directs that activities involving the removal of wildlife are only permitted for registered units for the management of the conservation of wildlife, and they require previous authorization granted by the Ministry of the Environment.

§2. Legal Origin

404. The Wildlife Act also regulates the traffic of specimens of wildlife or their parts. Thus, Article 50 states that, to grant authorization related to the transport, import, or export of specimens of wildlife or their parts, administrative Authorities shall check their legal origin.

405. Legal origin certifies that specimens of wildlife or their parts have been subjects of sustainable exploitation, as well as of the authorized rate. Legal origin appears in marks or in the appropriate receipts or invoices. Such marks must fulfil the requirements established by Federal Act of Metrology and Standardization.

406. A receipt or invoice must include the authorization number for exploitation; the data related to the place where the extraction of a specimen was authorized; the species and gender of that specimen, its parts, or sub-products; the authorized rate; the name of the person who authorized the action, and the proportion of the rate authorized for that the specimen that it, its parts, or sub-products represent.

§3. Areas for Protection of Wildlife Aquatic Species

407. Although the Wildlife Act's provisions are not applicable to aquatic species, in accordance with Article 65 of the Act, the Ministry of the Environment is authorized to establish, by issuing a Ministerial Regulation, areas for protecting aquatic wildlife species. These areas can be declared in waters under Federal jurisdiction and in terrestrial and marine Federal zones and wetlands, with the objectives of conserving and contributing to – through measures for management and conservation – the development of these species, as well as of preserving and protecting their habitats. To meet these objectives, the Ministry of the Environment shall elaborate 'protection programmes' for each one of these areas.

408. Because of their characteristics, these areas of refuge can duplicate the regulation that already establishes the Environmental Law in relation to the PNAs. In fact, Article 68 refers to this problem by stating:

> When the surface of one of the protected areas to protect aquatic species coincides with the polygon of a protected natural area, the respective protection program must be compatible with the general objectives established in the corresponding declaration and in the area management program Protection of the area.

409. On the other hand, as in the case of NPAs or critical habitats, declaring these areas of refuge involves limiting the development of works or activities. Article 69 of the LGVS deals with this aspect by pointing out:

> The execution of any public or private work, as well as those activities that may affect the protection, recovery and restoration of natural elements in areas of refuge to protect aquatic species, should be subject to the conditions that are established as management measures and Conservation programs in question, as well as the corresponding preventive report, in accordance with the regulations.

410. Given that most of the waters are nationally owned and the species of flora and fauna are an access to habitat, in this case of aquatic ecosystems, the establishment of these areas of refuge does not affect the right of private property but still requires adequate justification. In that regard, Article 67 provides:

> Prior to the issuance of the agreement, the Secretariat will prepare the supporting studies, which should contain, in accordance with the regulations, general information, diagnosis, description of the physical characteristics of the area, justification and socio-economic aspects; For which it may request the opinion of the competent Federal Public Administration units.

§4. Banned Seasons

411. In accordance with Article 71 of the Wildlife Act, when another mechanism for the conservation or recovery of populations of wildlife does not exist, the environmental authority will be able to limit their exploitation by establishing, modifying, suspending, or prohibiting exploitation activities during a period of time called a banned season.

According to Article 71 the imposition of banned seasons can be due to three causes:

(1) In case of natural disasters.
(2) At the request of interested natural or moral persons.
(3) By decision of the Ministry of the environment.

§5. Critical Habitats

412. Article 63 of The Wildlife Act grants to the Ministry of the Environment the authority to declare the existence of critical habitats for wildlife preservation in specific areas where: (a) there are species or populations at risk that can be preserved through the development of biological processes; (b) in spite of their destruction, these areas are still home to significant amounts of biodiversity; (c) endangered ecosystems are present; and (d) Specific areas in which essential biological processes are developed, and there are specific species sensitive to specific risks such as certain types of pollution, whether physical, chemical, or acoustic.

413. The same precept defines critical habitats as: those 'specific terrestrial or aquatic areas, where essential biological, physical and chemical processes occur, either for the survival of species in the category of risk, either for a species or for one of its populations, and therefore, require special management and protection' and adds that: 'These are areas that are regularly used for feeding, predation, foraging, resting, breeding or reproduction, or Migration routes.'

414. Article 64 of the Wildlife Act refers to the limitations that the right to property can impose the declaration of critical habitat. In this regard, first of all, the precept of rules contemplates the possibility of such limitations being agreed between the authority and the owner. The first paragraph of the article states: 'The Secretariat shall agree with the owners or legitimate owners of lands where there are critical habitats, special management measures, mitigation of impacts and conservation.'

415. However, the final paragraph of Article 64 contemplates the assumption that agreement between authority and owner is not possible and clearly establishes the authority of the State to expropriate the lands necessary for the constitution of the critical habitat. This paragraph states:

> At all times, the Federal Executive may impose limitations of the rights of dominion in the lands that cover such habitat, in accordance with articles 1, section X and 2. Of the Expropriation Law, in order to comply with the necessary measures for its management and conservation.

416. On the other hand, the same Article 64 defines the scope that has the limitations to the right of property that brings with the declaration of a critical habitat. This precept says:

> The carrying out of any public or private work, as well as those activities that may affect the protection, recovery and restoration of natural elements in critical habitats, should be subject to the conditions that are established as special management and conservation measures in the Management plans in question, as well as the corresponding preventive report, in accordance with what is established in the regulations.

§6. Authorizations for Taking Wildlife

417. The Wildlife Act does not prohibit the taking of wildlife elements, but it did establish a series of limits to this activity. First of all, section VII of this Act discriminates between two categories of taking wildlife: (a) extractive taking, and (b) non-extractive taking.

418. Extractive taking means, in terms of paragraph 1 of Article 3, the use of units, parts, or derivatives of wildlife specimens by collecting, capturing, or hunting such specimens, whereas non-extractive taking consists of those activities directly connected to the wildlife in its natural habitat that do not imply the removal of units, parts, or derivatives, and, should they not be suitably regulated, could cause significant impacts on biological processes, populations, or habitats for that wildlife species.

419. As a general rule, Article 82 holds that extractive taking is only possible under conditions of sustainability, and Article 83 points out that an activity for extractive taking requires previous authorization from the Ministry of the Environment, which shall establish the rate and temporality of such taking. Special authorization regimens are provided for specific cases:

- Authorization in cases of species at risk will be granted only if the priority activities to collect or to capture have as objectives restoration, repopulation, or reintroduction. Activities with any other objectives can be approved only if at least one of those activities is developed and two conditions are met: (a) the specimens are products of controlled reproduction, or (b) the specific taking of the specimens contributes to the development of populations by controlled reproduction (Article 85).
- In case of species that are not naturally placed in national territory and were under confinement, a statement must be presented to the Ministry of the Environment (Article 86).
- Taking for subsistence objectives does not require any authorization.
- Taking by sportive hunting can be authorized only in specific seasons (Article 94).

420. Finally, an authorization for non-extractive taking is also required to guarantee the welfare of wildlife elements, the continuity of their populations, and their habitat preservation (Article 99).

§7. Special Regime for Threatened Species

421. The term endangered species refers to those whose distribution areas or size of their populations in the National Territory have drastically reduced their biological viability throughout their natural habitat because of factors such as the destruction or drastic modification of Habitat, unsustainable use, diseases or predation, among others.[40]

422. Among the endangered species in Mexico we found 7 amphibians, 97 birds, 10 fungi, 17 invertebrates, 52 mammals, 81 fish, 187 plants, and 27 reptiles. Some of these species are for example, the sea otter, the ajolote, the Antillean manatee, the Mexican prairie dog, the rabbit of the volcanoes, the Mexican gray wolf, the jaguar, among others.[41]

423. Neither Mexican legislation nor the regulations deriving from it have fully protected endangered species. Only the General Law on Wildlife, the General Law on Ecological Equilibrium and Environmental Protection, the Fisheries Law, and the General Law on Sustainable Forest Development contain provisions on the subject.

424. Article 3, section XX of Wildlife Law, provides the definition of 'Species and populations at risk', indicating that they are those identified by the Secretariat as probably extinct in the wild, in danger of extinction, threatened, or subject to special protection. However, the core of this law is found in Articles 47, 47*bis*, 47*bis* 3, 58, and 87 last paragraph, which establish that the Secretariat will promote the development of the National System of Management Units for the Conservation of wild life, with

40. Norma Oficial Mexicana OMN-059-SEMARNAT-2010 2.2.2.
41. Norma Oficial Mexicana OMN--059-SEMARNAT-2010 *Anexo Normativo III Lista de especies en riesgo (regulatory anex III list of species in risk).*

the purpose of reinforcing their buffer zones and giving continuity to their ecosystems. The final part of the law refers to infringements (Article 122 f. IV) if exploitation activities are carried out with specimens or populations of endangered wild species.[42]

425. The concept that we analyse is found in different provisions of the Environmental Law. First, this law refers to species in danger of extinction in Article 35 that refers to the resolution of the manifestation of environmental impact, in fraction III b) provides that the requested authorization can be denied if as a result of the evaluated activity or work could cause that one or more species are declared as threatened or in danger of extinction or when one of these species is affected.

426. Reference is also made to the concept in relation to the establishment of protected natural areas (Article 45) and in the case of the establishment of vedas. Article 81 of Wild Life Law establishes that the purpose of the closures shall be the preservation, repopulation, propagation, distribution, acclimatization, or refuge of specimens, especially those endemic, endangered, and endangered species. And last, the law refers to the exploitation, which is divided into the use of 'natural resources in areas that are the habitat of species of wild flora and fauna' and in the use of 'species of wild flora and fauna in economic activities'. The first one states that it must be done in a way that does not alter the necessary conditions for the subsistence, development, and evolution of these species, while the second provides that no species of wild flora and fauna will be granted in economic activities and when granted shall not threaten or threaten the species (Articles 83, 87, and 89).[43]

427. The General Law on Sustainable Fisheries and Aquaculture only refers to the subject in its Article 13 that corresponds to the powers of the governments of the Federative Entities. Thus, in section XV d), the precept in question stipulates that they must participate with the competent dependencies of the Federal Public Administration in the determination of aquatic species subject to special protection, threatened or in danger of extinction.

428. Finally, in the General Law of Sustainable Forest Development the issue of species in danger of extinction is addressed from two perspectives. First, Article 33 establishes obligatory forest policy criteria, among which fraction XV establishes the priority conservation of endemic, threatened, endangered species or subject to special protection. Second, Articles 99 and 106 refer to the use of timber and non-timber forest resources, both of which stipulate the conditions for their realization in a way that does not affect the habitat of species in danger of extinction. It should also be noted that, in the final part of this Law, specifically in Article 128, section III, it is envisaged that forest closures may be enacted as an exceptional measure when they are intended for the conservation, repopulation, propagation, dissemination, acclimatization, or shelter of endemic, threatened, endangered, or protected species.[44]

429. Meanwhile, environmental regulations are not very clear. Regarding the protection of species of flora and fauna in danger of extinction, at the time they have been applicable to three Mexican Official Norms:

42. Ley General de Vida Silvestre.
43. Ley General del Equilibrio Ecológico y Protección al Ambiente.
44. Ley General de Desarrollo Forestal Sustentable.

(1) The Official Mexican Nomenclature OMN-059-ECOL-1994, which determines species and subspecies of terrestrial and aquatic flora and fauna in danger of extinction, threatened, rare, and subject to special protection, and which establishes specifications for its Protection, published in the Official Gazette of the Federation on 16 May 1994.
(2) Mexican Official Norm OMN--059-SEMARNAT-2001 Environmental Protection-Native Mexican Species of Wild Flora and Fauna-Risk Categories and Specifications for Inclusion, Exclusion, or Change-List of Species at Risk, published in the Official Gazette of the Federation on 6 March 2002. This standard replaced the previous one.
(3) Mexican Official Norm OMN--059-SEMARNAT-2010, Environmental Protection-Native species of Mexico of wild flora and fauna-Categories of risk and specifications for inclusion, exclusion, or change-List of species at risk, published on 30 December 2010. This Standard replaced that of 2001.

430. The Mexican Official Mexican Norm of 1994, as provided by its numeral 1, had a double object. On the one hand, to identify species and subspecies of terrestrial and aquatic flora and fauna in danger of extinction, threatened, rare, and those subject to special protection and, on the other hand, to establish specifications for their protection.

431. However, compliance with the first objective referred to the provisions contained in paragraphs 3.6.1–3.6.4 that established the categorization of the flora and fauna in:

(1) Species and subspecies in danger of extinction.
(2) Threatened species and subspecies.
(3) Species and rare subspecies.
(4) Species and subspecies subject to special protection.

Numeral 5 of the standard complemented the aforementioned because it enlisted the species present in the national territory, identifying their status according to the aforementioned classification.

432. On the other hand, the establishment of specifications for the protection of these species is an issue that was developed in numerals 6.1–6.6.

433. Numeral 6.1 refers to the extraction of the natural environment from specimens, parts, products, by-products, or derivatives of endangered, threatened, rare species, and subspecies of terrestrial and aquatic flora and fauna and those subject to special protection for purposes of scientific collection, establishing as main regulations two: (a) the necessary authorization, and (b) the prohibition of its commercialization.

434. Numeral 6.2. refers to the extraction of specimens or parts of endangered, threatened species and subspecies of endangered terrestrial and aquatic flora and fauna and those subject to special protection under permanent closure for the purpose of being used as breeding stock, Mother plant, seeds, or propagules for the creation of breeding units. This activity was subject to authorization by the authority. In the same way was the provision of specimens or parts of species and subspecies of terrestrial and aquatic flora and fauna in danger of extinction, threatened, and those subject to special protection under permanent closure.

435. Numeral 6.3 refers to the commercial use, possession, or use of species and subspecies, their parts, products, and by-products of rare terrestrial and aquatic fauna and flora and those subject to special protection with a temporary ban or without a ban. The regulation that established the rule with respect to these activities consisted in the fact that they should be done on specimens coming primarily from authorized breeding units of wild flora and fauna (AMU).

436. Numeral 6.4. Authorizes the commercial exploitation, possession, or use of species and subspecies, their parts, products, and by-products of rare terrestrial and aquatic fauna and flora and those subject to special protection without a ban, in their natural environment. This authorization is subject to the availability rates determined by the Secretariat.

437. Numeral 6.5 refers to the use or use of habitats in which species and subspecies of terrestrial and aquatic flora and fauna, which are in danger of extinction, threatened, rare, and those subject to special protection, are found within these categories. Endemic to the Mexican Republic and waters under federal jurisdiction.

438. Numeral 6.6. It simply points out who was responsible for granting authorizations for the extraction of the natural environment or for the marketing of specimens, parts, products, by-products, and derivatives of species and subspecies of terrestrial and aquatic flora and fauna, but does not add any regulation.

439. For its part, NOM-059-SEMARNAT-2001 also has a double objective but differs from that of 1994. In other words, this norm pursues to:

- identify the species or populations of wild flora and fauna at risk in the Mexican Republic by integrating the corresponding lists, as well as,
- establish criteria for inclusion, exclusion, or change of risk category for species or populations, through a method of assessing their extinction risk.

440. As noted, OMN-059-SEMARNAT-2001 was no longer concerned with establishing criteria for the protection of the species in question, but only with its classification. Moreover, the OMN states in paragraph 2 that it is mandatory for 'all natural or moral persons that promote the inclusion, exclusion or change of wild species or populations in any of the categories of risk In the national territory, established by this rule'. Therefore, that rule did not establish any regulation regarding the protection of species to which it refers, from which it follows that it was the intention of the Federal Government to repeal that protection regime.

441. Finally, OMN -059-SEMARNAT-2010, Environmental Protection-Mexico's native species of wild flora and fauna-categories of risk and specifications for inclusion, exclusion or change-List of species at risk 2010 is outlined as a target in its Numeral 1 that says:

> identify the species or populations of wild flora and fauna at risk in the Mexican Republic, by means of the integration of the corresponding lists, as well as to establish the criteria of inclusion, exclusion or change of category of risk for the species or populations, by means of a method Of its risk of extinction and is

> mandatory throughout the National Territory for natural or moral persons that promote the inclusion, exclusion or change of wild species or populations in any of the categories of risk established by this Standard.

442. In other words, like its predecessor of 2001, no longer refers to specific regulations on the species of flora and fauna but only to its classification and integration in its case within the categories established by it.

443. Consequently, neither Official Mexican Standard OMN -059-ECOL-1994, nor OMN -059-SEMARNAT-2001, nor OMN -059-SEMARNAT-2010, currently in force, protect in themselves the species of wild flora and fauna and 'endangered, threatened, rare and subject to special protection', with respect to the realization of projects in their habitat, but simply indicate the criteria that regulate the inclusion or exclusion of these species within each of the categories of protection and, therefore, provide a conceptual basis for subsequent regulations to deal with the subject, but so far there is no legal provision prohibiting the carrying out of productive activities in places where species are located under status to which the standard refers.

Chapter 3. Agricultural Resources

444. The Agrarian Act regulates matters related to the use of land for agricultural purposes, whereas the Act for Sustainable Rural Development (Rural Development Act) has the objectives of promoting sustainable rural development and of providing a healthy environment, in accordance with Articles 4 and 25 of the Federal Constitution (Article 1o), by promoting the processes of social and economic transformation, recognizing that the vulnerability of rural populations leads to a sustainable and permanent encouragement of acceptable living conditions for these populations.

445. Nevertheless, it is only a statute that establishes the rules for planning actions from Federal and local governments to encourage the sustainability of economic activities for rural development.

446. Conservation and protection of national lands, including those destined for agricultural purposes, is governed by the Rural Development Act. The Agrarian Act regulates the creation and operation of various forms of agricultural communities, such as ejidos (communal village farmlands) and communities.

447. The Environmental Act establishes the general criteria and policies regulating soil use for the purpose of preserving and restoring the ecological balance. Article 98 sets forth the general principles for soil use regulation and provides that the soil is to be used in a manner compatible with its essential purpose, so that its physical integrity and productive capacity are not altered; practices that induce soil erosion, degradation, or other adverse environmental impacts must be avoided; restoration projects in areas of severe erosion or deforestation must be devised; and erosion preventing activities are to be implemented during the construction of public or private works. These principles must be considered by the federal government when adopting support programmes for agricultural activities, including investment, financing, and technical assistance.

448. Article 103 of the Act also requires that soil conservation and restoration practices necessary to prevent soil and environmental deterioration be implemented in connection with all farming activities. In areas of serious desertification and erosion, the Ministry of the Environment, in cooperation with other federal, State, and local Authorities, may design and implement special programmes regulating land uses and the exploitation of natural resources, with the aim of restoring the ecological balance. Notice of such programmes must be published in the *Federal Official Journal* previously to be implemented.

449. The Rural Development Act is intended to promote Mexico's sustainable rural development and an appropriate environment. The law applies to ejidos and rural communities and associations, as well as to individuals and entities that carry out rural activities.

450. The Act's objectives include the promotion of biodiversity conservation, the improvement of the quality of natural resources, and the furtherance of the Federal government's conservation and improvement of soils and other natural resources.

451. Under the law, support shall be given as needed to change production structures to re-orient land use in cases of high levels of erosion or negative ecosystem impact. In coordination with other sectors, the federal government shall also support the execution of soil and water conservation projects.

Chapter 4. Forests

452. In 2003, the Federal Congress passed the Forest Act, which, according to Article 1, has the following general objectives:

> I. Contributing to social, economic, ecological, and environmental development of the country through the sustainable management of forests, as well as basins and hydro-forest ecosystems;
>
> II. Promoting silviculture and the use of forest resources so that they provide goods and services that make possible the improvement of quality of life of Mexicans, particularly landowners and people living in forests;
>
> III. Developing natural resources and environmental services provided by forest resources and protecting, preserving, and increasing biodiversity;
>
> IV. Promoting the organization, operative capacity, integrity, and professionalism of public institutions from Federal, local, and municipal governments for sustainable forest development; and
>
> V. Respecting the right to use and enjoy forest resources in places inhabited by indigenous communities, in accordance with Article 2, section VI of the Mexican Constitution and other applicable legal provisions.

453. This Act grants ownership of the forests to the holders of the lands (communities, towns, private persons, corporations, government, localities, etc.) where forests are located. Article 5 of the Forest Act states that property of forest resources placed in national territory corresponds to ejidos, communities, towns and indigenous communities, natural and juridical persons, federations, estates, Federal districts, and municipalities that own lands where forests are located.

454. Nevertheless, the exploitation of forests is subject to a series of controls established by the Forest Act. First of all, Article 73 of the Forest Act states that:

> Exploitation of timber in forest lands or a land with preferential forest allocation requires authorization granted by the Ministry of the Environment. Such authorization shall include the management program authorization referred to by this Act and the one that corresponds to granting it in regard to the environmental impact assessment, according to the applicable legislation.

455. Second, according to Article 76 of the Forest Act, a forest management programme must be attached to a request for authorization for timber exploitation.

Article 76 of the Forest Act establishes that an environmental impact statement is required in cases of:

I. forest exploitation in rain forests greater than 20 hectares (3,412.8 feet);

II. forest exploitation of species of difficult regeneration; and

III. forest exploitation of protected natural areas.

456. In accordance with Article 77 of the Forest Act, to obtain an authorization for timber exploitation in land surfaces equal to or less than 20 hectares, a simplified forest management programme for each piece of land or for a group of pieces of land that together do not exceed 250 hectares (26,910 feet) must be attached to a request for authorization. A standard forest management programme is required in cases of exploitation of land surfaces equal to or greater than 20 hectares but smaller than 250 hectares. Finally, when a land surface to be exploited is greater than 250 hectares, an advanced level of a forest management programme is required.

457. Article 76 of the Forest Act also provides that the environmental impact statement shall be incorporated into the forest management programme so that only one administrative procedure is conducted.

458. In addition to forest exploitation authorization, the Forest Act requires authorization granted by the Ministry of the Environment in the following cases:

(a) land use changes in forest areas (Articles 58 and 117);
(b) the establishment of commercial forest plantations in surfaces greater than 800 hectares except those in temporary forest lands (Articles 58 and 92); and
(c) collections and uses of genetic resources with commercial aims or for research (Articles 58 and 101).

459. Besides the traditional methods of direct regulation, the Forest Act also refers to a series of innovative methods for stimulating forest conservation, such as: (a) the conservation bonus, (b) the environmental services market, and (c) the Forest Fund. Nevertheless, these mechanisms are not linked to each other so as to meet the objective of protecting the commodities and environmental services delineated by Article 2, paragraph III.

460. Article 114 of the Forest Act refers to the certification of good forest management as a mechanism to certify suitable management of forests, to improve the protection of forest ecosystems, and to make easier the access to the national and international markets of environmental services.

461. According to this Provision, the Forest Commission shall promote the certification of good forest management so that the forest owners can obtain the required certificate.

462. Furthermore, Article 141 adds that the bonus has the objective to certify forest conservation so as to enable the forest owner or possessor to be paid for the environmental commodities and services generated.

463. Complementing this concept, Article 133 of the Forest Act establishes that 'in accordance with international treaties as well as national law, the Ministry of Environment shall promote the development of a market of environmental commodities and services that compensates the benefits provided by the landowners and possessors of forest resources to other sectors of society'.

464. Additionally, Article 134 states that the Ministry of the Environment shall encourage the capacity of buildings to enable professionals, technicians, and companies to certify, to evaluate, and to monitor environmental commodities and services, as well as to provide technical assistance and training to the holders of authorizations for forest exploitation and to connect them with the users or beneficiaries of the environmental commodities and services, as well as with the corresponding markets within national and international scopes.

465. Finally, Article 142 created the Mexican Forest Fund as the instrument to promote conservation, increasing sustainable use and restoration of forest resources and resources associated with them by facilitating access to financial services in the market, impelling projects that contribute to the integration and competitiveness of the productive chain and to the development of mechanisms for collecting and paying for environmental commodities and services.

466. According to the Forest Act, the Mexican Forest Fund will operate through a mixed committee that gathers representatives from public and social sectors, as well as from the private organizations of forest producers.

467. In accordance with Article 143 of the Forest Act, the Mexican Forest Fund revenues come from the following:

(a) Federal, local, and municipal contributions;
(b) Loans and national and international organizations;
(c) Contributions and donations from private, mixed, national, or international Corporations;
(d) Taxes on forest products imports;
(e) Profits from the operation and investment of free funds in commercial and governmental bonuses;
(f) Five per cent of the certificated bonus value, referenced by Articles 114 and 141 of the Forest Act;
(g) Payments for commodities and for environmental services and technical assistance;
(h) Transfers of revenue from users of hydrological basins; and
(i) Resources coming from other sources.

468. The role of the Fund is not completely clear in the Forest Act, but taking into account the content of Article 143, it is possible to infer that the Fund acts as a collector of the payments for environmental services so as to transmit the collected resources directly to the suppliers of those services, that is, the forest owners or possessors. Nevertheless, this provision does not limit the possibility of contracts being signed directly between a supplier and consumer of environmental services.

469. It is important to mention that, in accordance with the aforementioned Provision, payments for environmental services are deductible from income tax.

470. Other mechanisms considered by the Act to support the forest policy in Mexico include the following:

I. Planning of Forest Development;

II. The National System of Forest Information;

III. The National Forest and Soils Inventory;

IV. The Forest Zoning;

V. The National Forest Register;

VI. The Mexican Official Norms; and

VII. The National System for Forest Management.

Chapter 5. Fish Resources

471. The General Act for Sustainable Fishing and Aquaculture (Fishing Act) was passed by the Federal Congress in 2007. This is not really an Environmental Act. In fact, according to Article 1, it has the general objective of regulating, encouraging, and managing the exploitation of fishing and aquaculture resources in Mexican territory and zones where the Mexican Nation exerts sovereignty and jurisdiction. Although Article 2 lists among its specific objectives, 'to establish the basis for the arrangement, conservation, protection, repopulation, and exploitation of the fishing and fishery resources, as well as the protection and rehabilitation of the ecosystems in which these resources are located', it includes very few specific regulations to protect aquatic ecosystems.

472. In fact, section III of Article 2 indicates among those objectives:

> To establish the bases for the management, conservation, protection, repopulation and sustainable use of fishery and aquaculture resources, as well as the protection and rehabilitation of the ecosystems in which these resources are found.

473. Notwithstanding the foregoing, the Act includes very few legal instruments aimed at achieving this objective. Among these instruments, Article 36 points out:

I. The fisheries management programs;

II. Fishing management plans; and

III. Concessions and permits.

474. However, regulation of these instruments is precarious. For instance, under Fishing Act, the private capture, exploitation, and culture activities involving the resources referred to in the Fishing Act are possible only through permits or concessions granted by Federal Authority (Articles 40 and 41 of the Fishing Act). Such permits or concessions may be cancelled if an ecosystem results in being adversely affected or is in risk of being adversely affected.

Chapter 6. Subsoil and Minerals

475. The Mexican Constitution refers to sub-soils and minerals from the following perspectives:

(a) Article 27 grants the Nation direct dominion over all natural resources located in the continental shelf and the submarine foundations of islands; all minerals and substances in veins, the mantle, and masses or deposits that are by nature distinct from the components of the ground; metallic minerals used in industry; precious stones; salts; and materials that may be used as fertilizers.
(b) Under the Mexican Constitution, the Nation has an obligation to promote the conservation of natural resources and the restoration of the ecological balance.
(c) Private parties may only participate in the exploitation and use of these natural resources through concessions granted by the Federal Executive.
(d) In addition, the Mexican Constitution grants the Federal Congress the power to legislate in the area of mining.

476. Mining activities are regulated under the Mining Law and the Regulations of the Mining Law, while wastes resulting from mining activities are governed by the Waste Act. Wastewater discharges resulting from mining activities are governed by the National Waters Law and the Regulations of the Waters Act. Finally, the Foreign Investments Act regulates foreign investor participation in mining concessions.

477. On the other hand, Mexican legislation on sub-soils and minerals includes the Mining Act (as amended in 1996), the Regulatory Act of the Constitution on the Oil Branch (1958), and the Regulatory Act of Article 27 of the Constitution on Nuclear Matters (1989). All of these Acts refer to the exploration and exploitation regimes for subsoil and mineral resources and, in cases where these are allowed, to the manner of granting the concessions for private investments.

478. In general, these Acts contemplate an environmental evaluation system as a mechanism to control negative environmental effects. Consequently, some of them expressly mention the obligation to evaluate the environmental impact of works or activities related to the use and exploitation of mineral and energy resources, while in others, these activities are included in the general reference to the obligation to evaluate the environmental impact of any work or activity that can affect the environment in one way or another.

§1. Mining Activities

479. The Mining Law regulates the exploration, exploitation, and benefaction of minerals and substances for industrial use; rare metals; mineral gems; rock salt and its by-products; products derived from the decomposition of rocks whose exploitation is mainly carried out through underground works; certain minerals and organic materials that may be used as fertilizers; certain solid fuels; and other resources identified by the Federal Executive.

480. Article 5 of the mentioned Law specifically excludes the following from the jurisdiction of the Mining Law: oil and solid, liquid, or gas hydrocarbons; radioactive minerals; substances in suspension or dissolved in groundwater; rocks or products resulting from their decomposition used as building materials or in construction; products derived from the decomposition of rocks whose exploitation is mainly carried out by means of open-pit works; and salt from salt mines formed in interior basins.

I. Mining Concessions

481. Under Article 10 of the Mining Law, mining activities are carried out under concessions granted by the Secretary of Energy. Such concessions can be granted exclusively to Mexican nationals, ejidos, and agrarian communities, the towns and indigenous communities mentioned in Article 2 of the Mexican Constitution, and Corporations constituted under Mexican laws. There are two types of mining concessions: exploration concessions and exploitation concessions.

482. According to Article 11 of the Mining Law, the following are Corporations eligible to obtain mining concessions under Mexican laws: (a) those whose social objective refer to exploration or exploitation of minerals or substances regulated by the Mining Law, (b) those who have their legal addresses in the Mexican Republic, and (c) those in which participation of foreign investors fulfil legal provisions in that regard.

483. Under Article 13 of the Mining Law, mining exploration concessions are generally granted by the Secretary of Energy to whoever submits the application first. According to Article 15 of the Mining Law, mining concessions are granted for a renewable fifty-year term as of the date that they are registered in the Public Register of Mining.

484. A concession or assignment does not grant property rights over a land surface, but rather the right to explore and exploit minerals and substances that are different from the components of the soil.

II. Mining Assignments

485. Article 10 of the Mining Law also refers to mining assignments. Mining assignments are issued only to the Mineral Resource Council and strictly for the purpose of identifying and quantifying the potential mineral resources in a given area.

486. Mining assignments are granted for non-committed lots on free ground and may only be issued by the Secretary of Energy to the Mineral Resource Council. Mining assignments confer rights and obligations and have a non-renewable duration of six years as of the date that the title is published in the *Federal Official Journal*.

III. Mining Reserves

487. Finally, Article 10 of the Mining Law points out that, because of causes of public utility or for satisfying future necessities of the country, mining reserves can be established through an Executive decree. In the areas included in mining reserves, no concessions or assignments can be granted. According to Article 17 of the Mining Law, when the circumstances that motivated the incorporation of a given zone into a reserve zone have changed, the Executive shall declare its disincorporation through a decree that shall be published in the *Federal Official Journal.*

§2. Radioactive Substances and Minerals

488. Unlike the rights to other natural substances and minerals, the rights to explore, exploit, and use radioactive minerals cannot be granted through concessions or by contract. These activities are reserved exclusively to the State and are regulated under the Law Regulating Article 27 of the Constitution in Regard to Nuclear Matters. Under Article 5 of this Law, the properties of radioactive minerals are vested in the Nation, and the exploration, exploitation, and use of radioactive minerals, including the construction and operation of nuclear plants, is not a matter of concessions or contracts.

489. According to Article 9 of the Nuclear Matters Law, exploration activities may be exclusively carried out by the Mineral Resource Council[45] through assignments from the Secretary of Energy, whereas in accordance with Article 10, exploitation activities may be exclusively carried out by the Commission of Mining Promotion through assignments granted by the Secretary of Energy.

490. Finally, under Article 15 of the Nuclear Matters Law, the generation of electricity from the use of nuclear combustibles corresponds exclusively to the Federal Commission of Electricity. Nuclear energy can be used only for domestic objectives (Article 2).

491. The Secretary of Energy may determine the programme and technical conditions to be fulfilled by the Council in accordance with the relevant National Development Plans.

§3. Hydrocarbons and Petroleum

492. The original text of Article 27 of Mexican Constitution did not nationalize the oil industry. This precept established the principle of the public domain of

45. . In 2005, the Mineral Resources Council changed its name to Mexican Geological Survey.

hydrocarbons that was in force during colonial times,[46] but allowed the participation of private investment in the exploitation of oil resources.[47]

493. Fourth paragraph of Article 27 stated that the nation's dominion over hydrocarbon resources was inalienable and imprescriptible but at the same time sixth paragraph of such article authorized the federal government to grant concessions for its exploitation both to individuals and to legal entities constituted under Mexican law.[48]

494. The fourth and sixth paragraphs of Article 27 of the original text of the Political Constitution of the United States of Mexico, textually stated:

> The Nation has full ownership over all natural resources of the continental shelf and the seabed and subsoil of the submarine areas of the islands; over all minerals or substances in veins, layers, masses or ore pockets, constituting deposits which nature is different from the components of the earth, such as the minerals from which metals and metalloids to be used in industry are extracted; beds of precious stones, rock salt and deposits of salts formed by sea water; the products derived from rock decomposition, when their exploit requires underground work; minerals or organic deposits susceptible to be utilized as fertilizers; solid mineral fuels; petroleum and all solid, liquid or gaseous hydrocarbons; and the space located over national land territory, in the extension and under the terms established by International Law.
>
> In the cases established in the two paragraphs hereinbefore, the Nation's dominion is inalienable and not subject to the statute of limitation and the exploitation, use or enjoyment of the resources in question by private persons or by companies incorporated in accordance with Mexican laws, may not be undertaken save by means of concessions granted by the President of the Republic and in accordance with the rules and conditions set forth by the Laws.

495. In addition to the above, the Regulation of Article 27 of the Constitution in the Field of Oil passed by the Federal Congress in 1925[49] recognized the rights acquired by foreign oil companies based on the principle of non-retroactivity of the

46. *See* : Casafranca Valencia & Handersson Bady. *Ponencia sobre la propiedad de los recursos naturales en los territorios de pueblos indígenas Perú: La pobreza de los ricos territorios indígenas y recursos naturales* (2008). Available at: www.dar.org.pe/hidrocarburos.
47. In 1910, President Francisco Madero introduced a tax of 3 cents per barrel of oil and another of 20 cents per ton of oil extracted by private companies.
48. According to Raúl Jiménez, Art. 27 of the Mexican Constitution establishes a system of absolute ownership of the nation over hydrocarbons, as well as the direct and exclusive exploitation of these by the nation. Raúl Jiménez, *Historical Elements for the Interpretation of the Constitutional Regime of the Oil of the Mexicans*, in *Oil in the History and Culture of Mexico* 99–118 (Suárez del Real & Jose Alfonso Aguilera eds, PRD Parliamentary Group 2008).
49. DOF, 25 Dec. 1925.

Constitution of 1917[50] and detail regulated the regime of concessions that included the exploration, exploitation, and transportation of oil and other hydrocarbons.[51]

496. In 1934, the Supreme Court of Justice upheld this criterion by recognizing that Article 27 had no retroactive effect. Consequently, the 1925 Act, which established the procedure for private companies to request recognition of their acquired rights was, according to the Supreme Court of Justice`s absolute constitutional criteria.[52]

497. The first step on the road to the establishment of the absolute property regime of the oil state was given until 1938, when the Mexican government expropriated the facilities of the oil companies. However, even after the so-called oil expropriation, the absolute ownership principle of the state could not be said to regulate the petroleum property regime.

498. To nationalize the oil sector, it was necessary to introduce another principle in the constitutional text: the principle of the direct and exclusive exploitation of this resource by the nation. With this aim, in 1940 a constitutional reform was approved that modified the sixth paragraph of Article 27 in the following terms:[53]

> In the case of petroleum and solid, liquid, and gaseous hydrocarbons, no concessions or contracts will be issued and the respective regulatory law will determine the manner in which the Nation will carry out exploitations of those products.

499. Since that moment the Mexican government constitutionally assumed the monopoly of exploration, exploitation, refining, and distribution of oil and other products derived from it.

500. One year before, granting concessions was forbidden by a second Regulation of Article 27 in the Field of Petroleum. However, in spite of the constitutional reform, that Law was repealed in 1941 by a third Regulation of Article 27 in the Field of Petroleum that allowed the participation of private companies in the oil industry through the so-called contracts of risk. Under the 1941 Act, through these contracts, the exploration and exploitation activities could be carried out by private companies and the compensation for their services could consist of a cash payment or a percentage of the production obtained.[54]

501. Between 1949 and 1951 a number of contracts of risk were assigned to foreign companies.[55] These contracts included hydrocarbon resources in an area of 4,000 km^2 of national territory. The payment to the companies consisted in the total

50. For some writers, the enactment of this Law was the result of the 'Treaties of Bucareli' between Mexico and the United States. In these treaties, the United States of America recognized the government emanating from the Mexican revolution with the only condition that Mexico did not apply Art. 27 of the Constitution to the property titles granted by Porfirio Diaz to the oil companies.
51. *See* Arts 7, 8, and 9 of the mentioned Law.
52. *See The Eagle. Mexican Oil Company v. Government of Mexico*, 1934.
53. DOF, 9 Nov. 1940.
54. *See* : Mario Alberto Becerra Pocoroba, *Análisis de los aspectos más relevantes de la reforma energética* (2008). Disponible en http://www.senado.gob.mx/reforma_energética/content/foros/docs/20 de mayo2008_7.pdf.
55. In Bolivia, the Capitalization Act of 1996 introduced joint venture contracts for petroleum exploration and production.

reimbursement of their expenses and investments plus 50% of the value of the hydrocarbons produced by the drilled wells and a compensation of between 15% and 18% of the value of the production over a period of twenty-five years.[56]

502. Given that contracts of risk were signed in contravention of the constitutional principles defined in 1940 by the Constitution, in 1958 the Congress of the Union approved a fourth Regulatory Law of Article 27 of the Constitution in the field of Petroleum. The new law established the nation's ownership system over oil and other hydrocarbons in addition to the monopoly of public monopoly in the sector that included all activities related to the construction and operation of infrastructure.

503. The 1958 Law was an important step towards the configuration of a regime of absolute state ownership over hydrocarbons. This law prohibited for the second time the private participation in the petroleum industry. Article 2 established: 'only the nation can carry out the different exploitations that constitute the oil industry in the terms of the following article'. Article 3 complemented that provision by noting that the oil industry comprises the exploration, exploitation, refining, transport, storage, distribution, and first-hand sales and the products obtained from its refining; The exploration, exploitation, processing, and first-hand sales of gas, as well as the transport and storage essential and necessary to interconnect its exploitation and production.

504. A new step towards the nationalization of the oil industry was given in 1960, when the Constitution was amended again to indicate in the sixth paragraph of Article 27 that:[57]

> In the case of petroleum and solid, liquid or gaseous hydrocarbons, no concessions or contracts shall be granted, nor shall any such concessions be granted, and the nation shall carry out the exploitation of those products, in the terms prescribed by the regulatory law Respectively.

505. The 1960 reform also established that the direct domination of the nation over subsoil resources included the continental shelf, the seabed, and the submarine sockets of the islands.

506. Finally, in order to complete the constitutional process of nationalization of the oil industry, in 1982 Articles 25 and 28 of the Constitution were amended to establish that the oil industry is a strategic economic area and consequently a Mexican state monopoly, thus fully recognizing the regime of state ownership over oil and other hydrocarbons.

507. However, on the one hand, in 1995, a constitutional reform explicitly excluded the secondary petrochemicals from the state monopoly over the oil industry; And second, secondary legislation does not follow constitutional principles very closely, since the 1958 Act has been amended several times to allow private sector participation in this sector.

508. In May of 1995, the Federal Congress approved modifications to the Regulation of Article 27 of the Constitutional Act in the Field of Petroleum. This legal reform redefined the gas industry. It allows the private sector to build, operate, and

56. These contracts were cancelled in 1970 by the General Director of PEMEX, Jesus Reyes Heroles.
57. DOF, 20 Jan. 1960.

own systems of transport, storage, and distribution of natural gas. These activities were previously reserved to State regulation. The State keeps the power to regulate these activities. It also keeps the ownership of the natural gas itself and the operation of the public sector. As a complement to these modifications, the Regulation of Natural Gas was approved by the Executive. This Regulation defines three types of activities subject to governmental permission: transport, storage, and distribution.

509. By the end of the twentieth century, the oil industry was practically an absolute monopoly of the Mexican State. The only sub-sector of this industry that had been privatized was secondary petrochemicals. This happened by the reformation of the Federal Constitution in 1995. However, in 2008, the Regulation of Article 27, a Constitutional Act in the Field of Petroleum, was substantially modified to allow private investment in a number of activities regulated by this Act.

510. In 2013, Article 27 of the Mexican Constitution was amended, which preserves the direct, inalienable, and imprescriptible ownership of the nation, allows private participation in the exploration and exploitation of these resources, through the conclusion of contracts. The seventh paragraph of Article 27 of the Mexican Constitution provides as follows:

> In the case of oil and solid hydrocarbons, liquid or gaseous, in the subsoil, the property of the Nation is inalienable and imprescriptible and no concessions will be granted. In order to obtain income for the State that contributes to the long-term development of the Nation, it will carry out the exploration and extraction of oil and other hydrocarbons through assignments to productive enterprises of the State or through contracts with them or with private corporations, in the terms of the Regulatory Law. In order to comply with the purpose of such assignments or contracts, productive enterprises of the State may contract with individuals. In any case, the hydrocarbons in the subsoil are owned by the Nation and thus must be affirmed in the assignments or contracts.

511. However, according to Article Transitory Fourth of the Decree of constitutional reform commented on, the contracts that can be celebrated with the individuals are the following:

(1) Services;
(2) Of shared utility;
(3) Shared production;
(4) Licensing.

512. This brief analysis of the evolution of the constitutional and legal framework of oil and other hydrocarbons leads to the conclusion that while the reforms to the 1917 Constitution were aimed at establishing the model of absolute state ownership over these resources, subsequent reforms were evolving in the sense to recognize a model of national ownership in the terms defined at the beginning of this chapter, allowing private participation.

513. On 11 August 2014, the new Hydrocarbons Law (LH) was published in the DOF, which regulates Articles 25, fourth paragraph; 27, seventh paragraph; and

28, fourth paragraph of the CPEUM, regarding hydrocarbons. Article 1 of this regulation reiterates the constitutional principle according to which: 'The Nation shall be the direct, inalienable and imprescriptible propertary of all Hydrocarbons found in the subsoil of the national territory, including the continental shelf and the exclusive economic zone Located outside the territorial sea and adjacent to it, in mantles or deposits, whatever their physical state.'

514. For the purposes of this Law, trans-boundary deposits are those that are within the national jurisdiction and have physical continuity outside it. Also, any deposits or mantles outside national jurisdiction, shared with other countries in accordance with the treaties in which Mexico is a party, or under the provisions of UNCLOS, shall be considered as transboundary.

515. In accordance with Article 1, the material scope of application of the Hydrocarbons Law includes the following activities:

I. The Recognition and Surface Exploration, and the Exploration and Extraction of Hydrocarbons;

II. The Treatment, refining, alienation, commercialization, Transport and Storage of the Oil;

III. The processing, compression, liquefaction, decompression and regasification, as well as the Transport, Storage, Distribution, commercialization and supply to the Public of Natural Gas;

IV. The Transportation, Storage, Distribution, Marketing and Expend to the Public of Petroleum, and

V. Transportation by pipeline and Storage that is linked to Petrochemical pipelines.

516. Pursuant to Article 28 of the CPEUM, exploration and extraction activities for hydrocarbons are considered strategic and only the nation can carry them out. Article 5 of the LH reiterates this maxim. However, according to the constitutional text, the precept quoted adds that the nation will carry out both activities through assignees and contractors.

517. Accordingly, Title Two of the Law entitled 'Exploration and Extraction of Hydrocarbons and Recognition and Surface Exploration' regulates the way assignments are granted and contracts are executed. In addition to the foregoing, the second paragraph of Article 5 of the Law states that 'The activities of Recognition and Surface Exploration, as well as the activities referred to in fractions II to V of article 2 of this Law, may be carried out by *Petroleos Mexicanos*, any other productive enterprise of the State or parastatal entity, as well as by any person, prior authorization or permission, as appropriate, in the terms of this Law and its regulations,.'

Part III. Zoning and Land Use Planning

518. Land use is regulated by both, the Environmental Act and the Law on Human Settlements, Land Use Planning and Urban Development of 2016 (Urban Act).[58]

519. The Environmental Law regulates the ecological ordinance of the territory in the Second Section of the First Chapter of the First Title relating to 'Environmental Policy Instruments', whereas Urban Act rules urban planning.

520. The Environmental Act defines the ecological zoning plan of Mexican territory as 'the instrument of environmental policy that regulates or induces land use to protect the environment and to preserve and to exploit natural resources in a sustainable manner by analysing the deterioration trends and the potentialities for exploiting the land' (Article 3, paragraph XXIV); whereas according to fraction XXVI of Article 3 of the Urban Law, the territorial ordering of human settlements is 'a public policy whose purpose is the occupation and rational use of the territory as the spatial basis of socioeconomic development strategies and environmental preservation'.

521. The Environmental Act recognizes four levels of environmental planning: (a) Program of General Ecological Ordinance of the Territory (PGEOT), (b) Regional programmes for ecological ordinance, (c) Local programs for ecological ordinance, and (d) marine zone ecological ordinance programs.

522. The General Ecology Program of the Territory is issue by the Federal Executive. In accordance with Article 20 of the Environmental Law, it aims to establish:

> I. The ecological regionalization of the national territory and of the zones on which the nation exercises sovereignty and jurisdiction, based on the diagnosis of the characteristics, availability and demand of natural resources, as well as of the productive activities that develop in them and of the location and status of existing human settlements, and
>
> II. The ecological guidelines and strategies for the preservation, protection, restoration and sustainable use of natural resources, as well as for the localization of productive activities and human settlements.

523. Article 20 *bis* 3 of the Environmental Law states that the Regional programs for ecological ordinance must contain at least the following:

> I. The determination of the area or region to be ordered, describing its physical, biotic and socioeconomic attributes, as well as the diagnosis of its environmental conditions and the technologies used by the inhabitants of the area;

58. DOF 28 Nov. 2016.

II. The determination of the ecological regulation criteria for the preservation, protection, restoration and sustainable use of the natural resources that are located in the region in question, as well as for the accomplishment of productive activities and the location of human settlements, and

III. The guidelines for its execution, evaluation, monitoring and modification.

524. These programmes have to be issued by local state governments. However, the following cases participation of federal government is mandatory:

A) When an ecological region is located in the territory of two or more federative entities, the Federal Government, the respective States and Municipalities, and in the case of the Federal District, within the scope of their competencies, may formulate a regional program for ecological ordering but the Federation will celebrate the agreements or coordination agreements coming with the local governments involved.

B) When a regional Eco regional program includes a protected natural area, or part of the federation's competence, the program must be prepared and approved jointly by the Secretariat and the governments of the States, the Federal District and Municipalities In which it is located, as appropriate.

In accordance with Articles 20*bis* 4 and 20*bis* 5 of the Environmental Law, the local ecological ordering programmes are elaborated by the municipal authorities and must have the following objectives:

I. To determine the different ecological areas that are located in the area or region concerned, describing their physical, biotic and socio-economic attributes, as well as the diagnosis of their environmental conditions, and the technologies used by the inhabitants of the area.

II. To regulate, outside of the urban areas, the uses of the soil with the purpose of protecting the environment and preserving, restoring and making sustainable use of the respective natural resources, mainly in the accomplishment of productive activities and the location of human settlements, and

III. To establish ecological regulation criteria for the protection, preservation, restoration and sustainable use of natural resources within the urban areas, in order to be considered in the corresponding urban development plans or programs.

Marine zone ecological ordinance programs are formulated and issued by the Federal Executive and in accordance with Article 20*bis* 7 of the Environmental Law indicates that marine eco-management programs must contain at least:

> I. The precise delimitation of the area that will comprise the program;
>
> II. The determination of the ecological zones based on the characteristics, availability and demand of the natural resources included in them, as well as the type of productive activities that they develop, and
>
> III. Guidelines, strategies and other provisions for the preservation, protection, restoration and sustainable use of natural resources, as well as the carrying out of productive activities and other works or activities that may affect the respective ecosystems.

525. Similarly, the Urban Act establishes the following levels or planning: (a) the National Urban Development Programme, (b) local programmes for urban development, (c) programmes for zoning metropolitan areas, (d) municipal plans and programmes for urban development, (e) programmes for urban development in population centres, and (f) other plans and programmes derived from the aforementioned and considered by local laws.

526. Given that neither the Environmental Law nor the Urban Law are very strict in this regard, it can be argued that both laws are responsible for ordering the same territory, that is to say, the territory of the country as a whole. Although each of these mechanisms can be interpreted as ordering the national territory from two different points of view, ecological ordering does so from the point of view of productive activities, while urban planning does so from the point of view of human settlements. The fact is that neither law is clear in narrowing its spatial scope of application.

527. However, the reading of Article 22 of the Urban Law allows to assert that the territorial ordering of human settlements is limited to ordering the territory of population centres. When referring to the National System of Planning of Territorial Ordering, Urban and Metropolitan Development, this legal provision states:

> The planning, regulation and evaluation of the Territorial Ordering of Human Settlements and Urban Development of the Population Centres are part of the National Democratic Planning System, as a global, sectorial and regional policy that contributes to the achievement of the Objectives of the National Development Plan, federal programs and state and municipal plans.

528. On the other hand, the analysis of the Environmental Law allows to assert that the ecological ordinance of territory has supremacy on the urban order. The above based on the following reasons:

- The PGEOT establishes guidelines and ecological strategies for locating productive activities and human settlements (Article 20, section I).
- Regional Programs for Ecological Ordinance determine ecological regulation criteria for productive activities and the location of human settlements (Article 20a 3, section II).
- Programs or Ecological Ordinance establish the ecological regulation criteria to be considered by the corresponding urban development plans or programs (Article 20*bis* 4, section III).
- The urban planning programmes must be submitted to the environmental impact assessment procedure (Article 32 of Environmental Act).
- Urban development plans or programmes must take into account the guidelines and strategies contained in the ecological planning programmes of the territory (Article 23, section I).

Part IV. Liability Questions

Chapter 1. Private Law Liability

529. Mexican private law recognizes two types of liability: fault liability and strict liability. Fault liability is based on the existence of three elements: damage, a fault (illegal behaviour), and a link of causation between that conduct and the damage; strict liability, on the other hand, does not require proof of fault, although causation must still be established.

530. As the strict liability system was established as a link to dangerous activities involving a considerable level of risk, it has the potential to be applied to environmental damage. This explains why most Mexican environmental laws refer to the application of civil liability in cases of environmental damages.

531. For instance, Article 203 of the Environmental Act asserts:

> Independently from the criminal or administrative sanctions that proceed, all persons who contaminate or deteriorate the environment or affect natural resources or biodiversity shall be responsible and shall be forced to repair the caused damages, in accordance with applicable provisions of the Civil Code.

532. In the same way, Article 96*bis* (1) of the Waters Act points out:

> Individuals or Corporations that discharge residual waters, in violation to the legal applicable dispositions, and that cause contamination in a receiving body, shall assume the responsibility of repairing the environmental damage caused, independently of the application of the administrative, criminal, or civil sanctions that proceed, by means of the removal of the pollutants of the receiving affected body and to restore it to the state it was in before the damage took place, or when this is not possible, to pay compensation fixed in terms of Law by the Competent Authority.

533. Mexican environmental laws also establish a series of rules aimed at adapting the civil law system to the environmental field. Thus, in an attempt to avoid the problems of proving the link of causation in cases of environmental damage, Mexican environmental laws channel liability to a specific person. For instance, Article 152 of the Environmental Act states:

> Liability for the management and final disposition of hazardous wastes corresponds to those who generate them. In cases for which management services and the final disposition of the dangerous residuals have been hired out to companies authorized by the Secretary and the residuals are given to such companies, liability for the operations will be independent from the liability of the generators of the hazardous wastes.

534. In the same way, regarding restoration of damage, environmental laws recognize the priority of remediation over economic compensation. For instance, Article *152bis* of the Environmental Act sets forth the following:

> When the generation, management, or final disposition of dangerous wastes or materials results in soil pollution, those responsible for these operations will carry out the necessary actions to recover and to reestablish the conditions of the soil, so that it can be designated to some of the activities foreseen in the applicable program of urban development plans or of ecological zoning plans for such soils or areas.

535. In regard to damages caused to elements of wildlife or their habitats, Article 108 of the Wildlife Act points out:

> The restoration of the damage in the case of responsibility for damage to wildlife and its habitat will consist of the reestablishment of the conditions previous to the commission of this damage and, in cases in which such reestablishment is impossible, of the payment of economic compensation that will be dedicated, according to the Regulations of this Act, to the development of programs, projects, and activities linked to the restoration, conservation, and recovery of species and populations, as well as to diffusion, qualification, and surveillance.

536. In contrast, Article 136 of the Forest Act prioritizes the payment of economic compensation over restoration:

> In case of damages caused to forest resources, to the environment, to ecosystems, or to their components, the responsible party shall cover the corresponding compensation…independently of the application of administrative or criminal sanctions that proceed according to this law and other applicable legal provisions.
>
> The judges will be able to calculate the amount to be paid for damages caused to the ecosystems or third parties based on the established applicable legislation.

537. Finally, although the Waste Act does not establish the obligation of repairing environmental damage, it determines some approaches to carry out the restoration of polluted soils by residuals in Articles 78 and 79, which, respectively, point out:

> The Secretary, in coordination with the Secretary of Health, shall issue the Official Mexican Norms for the characterization of the polluted places, and it shall evaluate the risks to the environment and to health that derive from them, to determine, in conjunction with the risk, the restoration actions that shall proceed (Article 78).
>
> The Regulations on land use and the programs of ecological classification and of urban development shall be considered when determining the level of remediation of polluted places with dangerous residuals, based on the risks that will be avoided (Article 79).

538. In spite of adaptations of traditional civil liability rules by environmental laws, fundamental questions of liability for environmental damages are still unsolved, such as legal standing to bring actions to restore damaged environments. Only the Wildlife Act recognizes that, in cases of damages to wildlife or its habitat, it corresponds to the Environmental Prosecutor to bring actions aimed at restoring the damages. In the rest of the environmental laws, only the directly affected person has legal standing to bring an action.

539. In 2011, the Federal Congress started discussing the bill of Environmental Liability Act that was approved and came into force in 2013.[59]

540. This Law has fifty-six articles organized into three parts or 'Titles'. First Title named 'Of Environmental Liability' is the most important. It is comprised of Article 1 to Article 46. It is also divided into three chapters, as follows:

(1) Chapter One. *General provisions*. This chapter defines environmental damages and distinguishes between environmental and civil liability.
(2) Chapter Two. *Obligations derivate from causing environmental damages*. It states that those caused environmental damages are obliged to its reparation or when impossible to pay an economic compensation.
(3) Chapter Three. *Judicial procedure of environmental liability*. This chapter regulates: environmental actions; precautionary actions, burden of proof; and the scope of the final ruling. The chapter also creates an environmental compensation Fund.

541. Chapter One defines what is environmental damage and civil damage. Chapter Two is addressed to establish the legal consequence of environmental damage.

542. Second Title of the law regulates the alternative methods of Justice.

543. Finally, Third Title introducing some rules regarding criminal liability for environmental damages. Such rules complement provision of the Federal Criminal Code in this regard.

59. . *Supra*, 21.

Chapter 2. Criminal Law Liability

544. Environmental crimes are regulated by Title 25 of the Federal Criminal Code, called Crimes against the Environment and Environmental Management. This Title contains five chapters, four of which include twenty criminal conducts related to technological dangerous activities; biodiversity, biosafety; and environmental management; whereas Chapter 5 contains general provisions related to innovative penalties and precautionary measures to be adopted by judges when environmental criminal behaviour is committed.

545. The environmental crimes regulated by the Criminal Code include the following:

(a) Article 414 refers to the illicit management of hazardous substances.
(b) Article 415 refers to the illicit emission of pollutants into the air as well as illegal emissions of noise, vibrations, and thermal or light energy.
(c) Article 416 refers to the illicit discharge of pollutants to water or soil.
(d) Article 417 refers to illegal trafficking of forest materials and flora and fauna.
(e) Article 418 refers to the illegal destruction of natural vegetation, illegal causation of damage to forests, and illegal changing of land use into forest lands.
(f) Article 419 refers to illegal extraction, transportation, and transformation of timber.
(g) Article 420 refers to illegal and prohibited means of fishing and hunting; harm caused to marine mammals and sea tortoises; and illegal harm or trafficking of endangered species of flora and fauna, and genetic resources.
(h) Article 420bis refers to criminal harm to wetlands and illegal extraction of marine resources.
(i) Article 420 refers to illegal trafficking and management of genetically modified organisms.
(j) Article 420 refers to illegal actions against the public management of the environment.

546. Generally, making a person criminally liable implies a complex process. In accordance with the Mexican Constitution and the Federal Code of Criminal Procedure, to indict a person for a criminal violation, the prosecution must acquire enough evidence to sufficiently prove: (a) all of the elements of the specific crime committed, and (b) the probable participation of the person in the commission of the crime.

547. Additionally, environmental crimes contain various elements that must be proven. Pollution crimes are comprised of: (a) a specific action, such as the transport of hazardous wastes or the emission of pollutants into the atmosphere; (b) a harmful result, such as harm to public health, natural resources, wildlife, water quality, or ecosystems; and (c) the violation of an environmental statue, regulation, or legal standard, such as the discharge of pollutants into a river in a quantity that exceeds the statutory limits. Failure to obtain a regulatory permit and the Act of introducing a hazard into the environment may also be considered elements of a crime in some cases.

548. Under Mexican law, to indict a person for the commission of an environmental crime, the government must present evidence sufficient to demonstrate that a person purposely harmed the environment or possessed knowledge that such harm was possible. Under current regulations, criminal negligence is not sufficient to present an indictment for the commission of an environmental crime.

Chapter 3. Administrative Liability

549. All Mexican environmental laws have an established system of administrative sanctions to be applied in cases of non-compliance with the provisions of such laws. Thus, according to Article 161 of the Environmental Act, Article 104 of the Wildlife Act, Articles 158 and 160 of the Forest Act, Articles 101 and 102 of the Waste Act, and Article 86, paragraph V of the Waters Act, environmental authorities shall carry out actions to inspect and verify compliance with the provisions established in these Laws and Regulations. The Environmental Prosecutor and the National Waters Commission (NWC) are in charge of enforcing environmental laws in two ways: (a) by means of monitoring inspections, and (b) by imposing administrative penalties.

550. The administrative penalties for violations of Mexican environmental laws and regulations include fines, facility closings, and administrative arrests. The fines range from 20 to 50,000 times the minimum wage for the Federal District of Mexico at the time the penalty is imposed. The penalty may result in approximately the equivalent of USD 2,500,000. Sanctions consist of administrative fines, facility closings, arrest, insurance, suspension of authorizations, and so on.

551. A facility may be completely or partially closed through a facility closing or through a revocation of a business operations permit. An administrative arrest may require the violator to remain under arrest for up to thirty-six hours.

Part V. Juridical Actions of Individuals

Chapter 1. Administrative Remedies

§1. The Right to Access to Information

552. The right to access to environmental information is recognized by Mexican legislation in three ways. First, under the Environmental Act, any person can claim access to environmental information in the procedure of environmental impact assessment. In this regard, Article 34 of the Environmental Act points out:

> Once the Secretary receives a manifestation of environmental impact and integrates the file referred to by Article 35, it will put the file in the public's disposition so that can be consulted by any person.

553. Second, Articles 159, 159*bis* 1, and 159*bis* 2 oblige the environmental authorities to gather, organize, and make accessible to the public environmental information; whereas Article 159*bis* 3 gives all people the right to access information.

554. Finally, in 2002, the Federal Act of Transparency and Access to Information (Access to Information Act) was passed by the Federal Congress. According to Article 1, this Act has the objective of guaranty to people the right to access to information that governmental offices possess. This Act also created the Federal Institute for Access to Information as an autonomous entity in charge of promoting the right to access to information; to deny requests of information, and to protect personal data that governmental offices possess. Thus, based on this Act, access to information about environmental matters is much more comprehensive.

§2. Public Participation

555. The right of the public to participate in decision-making processes is recognized in three ways as well. First, the Environmental Act contains a specific chapter that addresses the regulation of public participation. According to this chapter, environmental authorities are obliged to promote public participation in the planning, executing, evaluating, and monitoring of public policies on the environment and natural resources.

556. Second, as mentioned in the previous section, public participation is allowed in the procedure of environmental impact assessment. Article 34 of the Environmental Act set up the Ministry of the Environment, so that, upon the request of any persons from the affected community where a project is planned to be constructed, it can organize a public consultation so that these persons may propose measures for the prevention or mitigation of environmental impacts that the project could cause.

557. Finally, Mexican environmental law allows public participation in the process of the approval of Mexican Official Norms (MONs).

§3. Access to Justice

558. Administrative decisions issue by environmental authorities can be combated through three mechanisms:

(a) The appeal for review before the environmental authority according to Article 176 of the Environmental Act.
(b) The trial of Nullification before TFJFA.
(c) Injunction actions.

559. As mentioned above, legal standing to file actions to combat environmental authorities' decision is nowadays widely recognized in Mexico. Neither the Constitution nor legislations require to prove the existence of a direct legal standing, but they recognize the so-called legitimate legal standing to file such actions.

560. By the reform of 2010 Mexican Constitution provided foundation for collective actions. Third paragraph of Article 17 states:

> The Federal Congress shall to enact laws regulating collective actions. Such Laws shall to define their scope of application, judicial procedures and mechanisms for damage restoration. Federal Judges have exclusive jurisdiction on these procedures and mechanisms.

561. In the same vain, in 2011 Article 107 of Constitution was reformed to provide foundation for filing injunctions action to protect, not only direct and individual legal interests, but also legitimate and direct interest.

'**Article 107**. All dispute considered under Article 103 shall be subject of the proceeding and formalities established by the law, in accordance with the following bases':

> I. 'The amparo trial must always be initiated at instance of injury party, having this character those who argument to have a right or individual or collective legitimate interest, under the condition that the act claimed violets a right recognized by this Constitution and with that it its juridical interest directly or because its especial legal situation.'

562. On its side, the Environmental Act recognizes the legitimate interest in Article 180 when saying:

> ARTICLE 180. – In the case of works or activities that violate the provisions of this Act and those to which it is supplementary applied and regulations and NOMs arising therefrom, ecological management programmes, the declarations protected natural areas or regulations and official Mexican norms derived from it, the individuals and entities with a legitimate interest has the right to challenge administrative acts relating thereto and the requirement to carry out the necessary actions to be observed applicable legal provisions, provided that they prove in the process that those works or activities cause or may cause damage to the environment, natural resources, wildlife or public health.
>
> To this end, optionally may lodge administrative review to be in this Chapter, or go to the Federal Court of Fiscal and Administrative Justice.
>
> For the purposes of this article, have a legitimate interest individuals or corporations of the communities potentially affected by such works or activities.

§4. Denuncia Popular (Popular Complaint)

563. Article 189 of the Environmental Act provides that any individual or group may report to the Environmental Prosecutor, through a *denuncia popular* (popular complaint), any matter that could result in harm to the environment or natural resources, or that violates any environmental law or regulation. According to this Provision:

> Any individual, social group, non-governmental organization, association, and partnership may denounce with the Federal Attorney General's Office or other Authorities, any fact, action, or omission producing or that may produce ecological imbalance or damages to the environment or to natural resources, or in violation of the Provisions of this Law and the other laws regulating matters related to environmental protection and preservation and restoration of ecological balance.
>
> If within the place in question there is no representative of the Federal Environmental Protection Agency, such denunciation may be filed with the municipal Authority or, at the option of the complainant, with the closest representative office of such agency.
>
> If the denunciation was filed with a municipal Authority and the same falls within Federal jurisdiction, it shall be sent to the Federal Environmental Protection Agency.

Chapter 2. Judicial Remedies

564. The Judiciary Branch participates in enforcing environmental law when people: (a) appeal an environmental impact assessment authorization, (b) file a constitutional *amparo*, or (c) file a civil suit.

§1. Administrative Motions for Appeal

565. Article 176 of the Environmental Act states:

> The final resolution issued in administrative procedures due to the enforcement of this Law, its Regulations, and provisions derived therein, may be appealed by the affected parties by: (a) filing a motion for review whiting fifteen working days counted from the day of the notice, or (b) through the Nullification action before the Federal Court of Tax and Administrative Justice.

§2. Amparo

566. In 1999, the Mexican Constitution was amended to recognize the so-called right to a healthy environment. Since this provision was included in the chapter of fundamental rights, based on such amendment, it was possible to argue that such constitutional reform made possible to bring an amparo action (injunction) in cases for which the Authorities' decisions affect this right.

567. However, the new Law on Amparo, regulating Articles 103 and 107 of the Political Constitution of the Mexican United States (as amended in 2011) recognizes the legitimate interest to file the injunction establishes that:

> ARTICLE 5. The parties to the injunction: I. The complainant, having such a character who claims to be the holder of a subjective right or a legitimate interest individual or collective, always claiming that the standard, act or omission claimed violated the rights provided in Article 1 of this Act and thereby produce a real and current involvement to their legal rights, either directly or by virtue of their special situation facing the legal system.
>
> Simple interest, in any case, may be invoked as a legitimate concern. The public authority may not invoke legitimate interest.

568. Thus, nowadays it is clearly possible to file an amparo action in defence of human right to a healthy environment. An *amparo* suit is a legal action, founded in the Mexican Constitution, in which an individual may seek damages for, or the suspension or annulment of, an Act by a government Authority that violates the individual's rights. An *amparo* suit may not be brought by an environmental organization on behalf of an affected group, or as a class action on behalf of many similarly situated individuals. Rather, it must be brought by an individual petitioner who can show that he or she has been affected directly and has suffered harm caused by the official action.

§3. Civil Suits

569. During the last two years, important changes have occurred in Mexican legal system aimed at wildly recognizing the legal standing to file actions for environmental damages.

570. First, the Federal Code of Civil Procedure was amended in 2011 to introduce the 'collective Actions' to protect collective rights such as the right to a healthy environment.

571. In this regard, Article 578 of the Federal Code of Civil Procedure asserts that Protection and defence of collective rights and interests are allowed in environmental matters.

572. Article 585 of the Code recognizes legal standing to file collective actions in environmental matters to:

(a) The Attorney General Office for Environmental Protection.
(b) A representative of at least thirty people affected for the environmental damage.
(c) NGOs.
(d) The Attorney General.

573. Second, in 2013 a new Federal Environmental Liability Act was passed by the Federal Congress.

This Law is regulatory of Article 4 of the Constitution and, therefore, its objectives are to guarantee the human rights to a healthy environment and the human right to challenging responsibility for environmental damage. To achieve its objectives, the Federal Environmental Liability Law regulates the environmental liability arising from damages caused to the environment, as well as restoration and compensation of such damages (Article 1).

574. Therefore, this Law is applicable only when three circumstances coincide:

(1) the existence of an environmental damage, and
(2) liability can be channelled through the federal judicial proceedings provided for by Article 17 of the Constitution, --that is to say through collective actions; alternative dispute resolution mechanisms; administrative procedures; or
3. environmental damage is the consequence of crimes against the environment or against environmental authorities.

575. The Federal Environmental Liability Act defines environmental damage in Article 2, third fraction as:

> The adverse and measurable loss, change, detriment, impairment, or alteration of habitats, ecosystems, natural elements and resources, their chemical, physical

or biological conditions, the interaction relationships between them, and of the environmental services they provide.

576. However, definition on environmental damage is not entirely clear, since it does not state at what point the adverse change, deterioration, impairment, affectation, or modification becomes into damage. Nor is it clear because it confuses the damage that occurs on environment as a subject of legal protection in itself with the damage that affects the natural elements that make it up. Moreover, it confuses pollution with environmental damage.

577. This lack of legal certainty generated by an inadequate wording of the cited provision may make it more difficult to comply with this Law. In addition to adding insult to injury Article 6 states that there is not environmental damage when the impairments, losses, affectations, modifications or deterioration are not adverse, due to the fact that:

(1) They have been expressly stated by the responsible and explicitly identified, delimited in their scope, evaluated, mitigated and compensated by conditions, and authorized by the Secretariat, prior to carrying out the conduct that originates them, through environmental impact assessment or its preventive report, the authorization of change of use of forest land or some other similar authorization issued by the Secretariat.
(2) They do not exceed the limits established by Environmental laws and Mexican Official Norms.

578. Consequently, in the case of these two cases, although there is in fact an environmental damage, the system of liability that the Law regulates will not be applicable and, therefore, restoration will not be possible under the Federal Environmental Liability Act.

579. The exception set forth in section I of Article 6 has another exception, since the last paragraph of this provision states that 'The exception provided for in section I of this article shall not operate, when the terms or conditions of the Authorization issued by the authority.'

580. Disregard for fundamental principles of law reaches its maximum when this law states in Article 7 that:

> In order to grant certainty and to induce economic agents to bear the costs of damages caused to the environment, the Secretariat should gradually issue Official Mexican Norms, which have the purpose of establishing case by case and subject to the Law of the matter, of deterioration, loss, change, impairment, affectation, modification and contamination, necessary to consider them as adverse and harmful.

581. The criteria established by the quoted provision is wrong. In traditional liability regimes the plaintiff must prove the evidence of damage whereas the defendant has to demonstrate that plaintiff's proofs are not sufficient to channelling liability. It corresponds the judge to decide on the damage existence. Conversely, this law grants the Ministry the power of defined whether the damage exits.

582. The same legal provision adds that:

> To this end, it will be ensured that these amounts are significant and are considered, among other criteria, the capacity of regeneration of natural elements. Failure to issue the rules referred to in the previous paragraph shall not impede or exempt the person responsible from their obligation to repair the damage to their base state, taking into account the concept provided for in article 2, section III, of this Law

583. In other words, the Congress of the Union vested the administrative authority with the power to decide when there is and when there is not environmental damage. This is absurd because environmental damage will exist whenever the balance between the environmental functions deprives the environment of its capacity to be an adequate support of life but not when an administrative authority decides it.

584. One positive aspect is that Article 4 of this law recognizes that environmental damage is different from the civil damage caused to natural resource owners, which is already regulated in the Civil Codes, and also points out that environmental liability is different from administrative or criminal liability. However, it never manages to delimit the borders of environmental damage and, therefore, fails in its objective.

585. The Environmental Liability Act recognizes three mechanisms for environmental damage restoration: (a) reparation *in natura*, (b) substitute reparation *in natura*, and (c) economic compensation, when it states in its Article 10 that any natural or collective person that with its action or omission directly or indirectly causes damage to the environment, will be responsible and will be obliged to repair the damages, or, when the repair is not possible to the appropriate environmental compensation.

586. Reparation *in natura* involves returning things to the state they were in before the damage occurred. As stated in Article 13 of the Federal Environmental Liability Act, reparation of environmental damage will consist of restoring to its base-state the habitats, ecosystems, natural elements, and resources, their chemical, physical, or biological conditions and the interaction relations between them, as well as the environmental services they provide.

587. Although this principle is desirable, it is difficult to carry out in practice, for it is necessary to know what the original state of the environment was, and this information is not always available and, on the other hand, the LFRA does not define legal instruments that allow arriving at such certainty.

588. In an attempt to deal with this problem, the mentioned legal provision states that restoration *in natura* is achieved through restoration, treatment, recovery, or remediation which is obviously tautological and confusing because it leads us to the absurd of asserting that environmental damage is repaired by repairing it.

589. Article 13 indicates a series of principles that govern the reparation of environmental damage. These principles are:

A) The repair must be carried out in the place where the damage was produced.

B) Land owners or possessor of lands where the environment has occurred, must allow restoration, in accordance with this Law. Failure to comply with this obligation will result in the imposition of the means of arrest and the criminal responsibility that Match.

C) Land owners or possessor of lands who are affected by the actions of environmental restoration when damage is caused by third parties, will have the right to file action against the person who is responsible for the damages caused to them.

590. On the other hand, *substitute reparation in natura*, consists of repairing an environmental damage similar to the one that is not susceptible of restoration. This mechanism for restoration of environmental damage is referred to in Article 17 of the Federal Environmental Liability Act. According to this provision, compensation for environmental damage will consist of the investment or actions that the responsible party does to generate environmental improvement, replacing total or partial restoration of the damage caused to the environment, as appropriate, and equivalent to the adverse effects caused by the damage. As in the case of in *restoration in natura*, the legal provision under analysis also establishes some criteria that govern *substitute restoration in natura*:

A) The investment or actions must be done in the ecosystem or ecological region where the damage has occurred.

B) If this is materially impossible, the investment or actions will be carried out in an alternative location, ecologically, and geographically linked to the damaged site and for the benefit of the affected community.

C) In the latter case, the criteria for priority sites for repair of damages, which the Secretariat may issue in accordance with the provisions of section 5, Chapter Three of this Title, shall apply.

D) The responsible may comply with the obligation set forth in this article, by contracting third parties.

591. The Federal Environmental Liability Act also refers to an economic sanction that, in accordance with Article 19, is not substitute, but an accessory to *restoration in natura* in any of its forms.

592. This pecuniary sanction will consist of the payment of an amount of money equivalent to:

> I. From three hundred to fifty thousand days of general minimum wage valid in the Federal District at the time of imposing the sanction, when the person responsible is a natural person, and
>
> II. From one thousand to six hundred thousand days of general minimum wage valid in the Federal District at the time of imposing the sanction, when the person responsible is a moral person.

593. Pursuant to Article 23 of the LFRA, the economic penalty will be determined by the judge taking into account the economic capacity of the person responsible for making the payment, as well as the limits, requirements, and guarantees provided in his favour by the Political Constitution of the United States of Mexico, the gravity of the damage caused and the intentional or negligent nature of the violation, ensuring that the economic benefit obtained, if any, is neutralized and the amount of the expenses of the actor or actors that have been necessary to prove responsibility. In each case, the court shall provide that the economic penalty is clearly sufficient to achieve the purposes of inhibition and general and special prevention referred to in Article 2, section XI of this Act.

594. The economic sanction to which we refer also is a mechanism for repairing environmental damage, although Article 2 of the same law states that the economic sanction consists of 'The payment imposed by the judicial authority to penalize unlawful conduct harmful to the purpose To achieve general and special prevention and to inhibit prohibited behaviour in the future', according to Article 46, that economic penalty is allocated to the Environmental Fund. This legal provision states:

> The Fund will be under the supervision, supervision and coordination of the Secretariat, and its patrimony will be integrated with:
>
> I. The economic penalty referred to in section XIV of Article 2. Of this Law, and
>
> II. The other resources obtained by any other concept, but expressly does not talk about compensation for damage.

595. However, in terms of Article 45 of the Federal Environmental Liability Act, the Environmental Liability Fund will have as its object the payment of compensation for damages caused to the environment, in the cases that the federal environmental authorities decide based on reasons of urgency or importance, as well as to pay for studies and researches requested by judges to the Ministry of the Environment or to the Attorney General's Office during the jurisdictional process of environmental liability. Therefore, the economic penalty is neither pecuniary compensation in the style of civil law, nor a fine in terms of administrative law, but a mechanism of general reparation for environmental damage.

596. Article 28 of the new Act grants legal standing to file actions for environmental damages to:

(a) Inhabitants of the community adjacent to the place where the damage occurred.
(b) Mexican non-profit private individuals whose corporate purpose is environmental protection in general, or any of its elements, when acting in representation of some inhabitant of the communities adjacent to the place where the damage occurred.
(c) The Attorney General Office for Environmental Protection.
(d) Local Environmental Prosecutors.

597. Supreme Court of Justice has ruled that Article 28 is unconstitutional because it reduces the scope of legal standing to non-governmental organizations that only can file actions on behalf of the directly affected communities but not in their own behalf; whereas Federal Code of Civil Procedure grants standing to such social organization in itself.

Selected Bibliography

Brañes Ballesteros, Raúl. Manual de Derecho Ambiental Mexicano. México: FCE/FUNDEA, 2000.

Cabrera Acevedo, Lucio. El amparo colectivo protector del derecho al ambiente y de otros derechos humanos. México: Porrúa, 2000.

Carmona, Lara. Ley General del Equilibrio Ecológico y la Protección al Ambiente. Comentarios y Concordancias. México: UNAM-PROFEPA, 2003.

De Aceves, Carla. Bases fundamentales del Derecho Ambiental Mexicano. México: Porrúa, 2003.

Delgado De Cantú, Gloria M. Estructuras política, económica y social. México, 2ª ed. Ed. Pearson Educación. 2003.

González Márquez, José Juan. Introducción al Derecho Ambiental Mexicano. México: UAM, 1999.

Gutierrez, Nájera, Raquel. Introducción al estudio del Derecho Ambiental. México: Porrúa, 1998.

Jímenez Cisneros, Blanca Elena. La contaminación ambiental en México. México: Limusa/Colegio de Ingenieros Ambientales, Instituto de Ingeniería de la UNAM/Femisca, 2001.

Mújica Álvarez, Violeta y Jesús FIGUEROA Lara. Contaminación Ambiental, causas y control. México: UAM, 1996.

Océano. Atlas Geográfico Universal y de México. Barcelona: Editorial Océano, 2004.

Selected Bibliography

Legislation

- Constitution of the Mexican United States, 1917
- Agrarian Act, 1992, as amended in 2008
- Act for Sustainable Rural Development, 2001, as amended in 2007
- Civil Code of the Federal District as Regards the Common Jurisdiction and for the Whole Republic as Regards the Federal Jurisdiction, 1928 (repealed)
- Federal Act to Prevent and to Control Environmental Pollution, 1971 (repealed)
- Federal Act of Environmental Protection, 1982 (repealed)
- Federal Act of Administrative Procedure, 1994
- Federal Act of Duties, 1981, as amended in 2008
- Federal Act of Metrology and Standardization, 1992, as amended in 2015
- Federal Act of the Sea, 1986
- Ecological Equilibrium and Environmental Protection General Act, 1987, as amended in 1996
- General Act of Wildlife, 2000
- General Act of Sustainable Fishing and Aquaculture, 2007
- General Act for Sustainable Forest Development, 2003
- General Act of Prevention and Integral Management of Waste, 2003
- General Act of Human Settlements, 1993, as amended in 1994
- Mining Act, 1992, as amended in 2006
- National Waters Act, 1992, as amended in 2008
- Sanitary Code of the United Mexican States, 1934 (repealed)
- Regulation under the Environmental Act in Regard to Environmental Impact, 2000
- Regulation Under the Environmental Act in the Field of Prevention and Control of the Pollution Originated by the Emission of Fumes and Powders, 1971
- Regulation Under the Environmental Act in the Field of Prevention and Control of Air Pollution, 1988
- Regulatory Act of the Constitution on the Oil Branch, 1958, as amended in 2008
- Regulatory Act of Article 27 of the Constitution on Nuclear Matters, 1985, as amended in 1998

Judicial Rulings (Jurisprudence)

Ecology – legal standing to file an injunction action against laws on that matter: it corresponds to the community as holder of the collective rights (legislation of the State of Mexico). The notion of legal standing is closely linked with the principle of relativity established by Article 107 of the Political Constitution of the Mexican United

States and with the effects of an injunction decision. Section II of the aforementioned Constitutional precept points out that 'the Judicial Ruling will always be such that it only refers to particular individuals, and it is limited to protect them in the specific case on which the injunction action refers without making a general declaration regarding the law or Act that motivated it'.

In the same way, when protection against a law is granted by the Judiciary, the effect of the decision is to protect the petitioner against the present and future application of such law, with the aforementioned principle of relativity being respected, as has been established by the High Court in the decision entitled 'Injunction Against Laws: The Effects of a Judicial Ruling That Grants the Protection Consists of Protecting the Petitioner Against Its Present and Future Application'. This means that the judicial body that grants the protection of the Justice of the Union will have a relative scope, given that it will be limited to only protect the petitioner that has initiated the respective trial, but not other people, being bound, therefore, to the declaration of unconstitutionality of the law to the specific case.

Article 9o of the Environmental Protection Act of the State of Mexico and Articles 1 section VIII, 15, sections I and II, 18, and 157 of the LGEEPA (effective in February of 1993) contain dispositions in ecological matters that refer to specific communities, establishing rights in favour of natural and juridical persons who integrate it and reside in those places, which could be considered as a collective right that gives to them collective legal standing so that a community by itself or by means of its legitimate representative can initiate the injunction trial.

From that perspective, when the injunction trial is initiated by an association whose existence does not consist of the safeguard of a right granted to it by the law when it is included in the legal hypothesis, but it consists of both the protection of a collectivity that is not represented by such association and of the enactment of a general declaration regarding the refuted law or ordinance, we have the case of the hypothesis described in section V of Article 73 of the Injunction Act; because if the protection is granted, the problem remains to determine the scope of the Judicial Ruling, which could not be other than those mentioned above and which would clearly conflict with section II of Article 107 of the Constitution, and that cannot legally happen. (No. Registro: 198,421. Tesis aislada. Materia(s): Administrativa, Común. Novena Época. Instancia: Pleno. Fuente: Semanario Judicial de la Federación y su Gaceta. Tomo: V, junio de 1997. Tesis: P. CXI/97. Página: 156. Amparo en revisión 435/96. Fundación Mexicana para la Educación Ambiental, A. C. 29 de mayo de 1997. Unanimidad de nueve votos. Ausentes: José de Jesús Gudiño Pelayo y Olga M. Sánchez Cordero. Ponente: Mariano Azuela Güitrón. Secretaria: Mercedes Rodarte Magdaleno.)

Suitable Environment for the Development and Well-Being Concept, and Regulation and Concretion of That Guarantee

Article 4, paragraph 5 of the Political Constitution of the Mexican United States added on 28 June 1999, the consecration of the right of all individuals to an appropriate environment for their development and well-being. In the same way, the preservation and restoration of the ecological balance and the protection of the environment in the National territory are regulated directly by the Constitution, given the great relevance that this matter has. In this sense, the protection of the environment and natural resources has such an importance that it is the 'social interest' of Mexican society, and it implies and justifies, when necessary, restrictions strictly necessary and intended to preserve and maintain that interest, precisely and specifically, in the laws that establish the public order. In this way, the Official Mexican Norm of Emergency MON-EM-136-ECOL-2002, protection of environmental specifications for the conservation of marine mammals in captivity, in paragraphs 5.8.7 and 5.8.7.1, prohibit the temporary or itinerant exhibition of cetaceans. From Articles 4o, paragraph 4, 25, paragraph 6, and 73, section XXIX(g) of the Federal Constitution, interpreted in a systematic and causal teleological way, and by principle, it is noted that they protect the right of people to an appropriate environment for their development and well-being, the appropriate use of natural resources, the preservation and restoration of the ecological balance, and sustainable development. The protection of an appropriate environment for development and well-being, as well as the necessity to protect natural resources and the preservation and restoration of the ecological balance, are fundamental principles that the Constitution has tried to protect and, although, this does not define in a concrete and specific way how this protection must occur, the definition of its content should be made based on a systematic, coordinated, and complementary interpretation of the legal provision that tends to meet, to figure out, and to promote the principles and fundamental values that inspired the Reform's power. (No. Registro: 179,544. Tesis aislada. Materia(s): Administrativa. Novena Época. Instancia: Tribunales Colegiados de Circuito. Fuente: Semanario Judicial de la Federación y su Gaceta. Tomo: XXI, enero de 2005. Tesis: I.4o.A.447 A. Página: 1799. Cuarto Tribunal Colegiado en Materia Administrativa del Primer Circuito. Amparo en revisión 28/2004. Convimar, S.A. de C.V. 26 de mayo de 2004. Unan-imidad de votos. Ponente: Jean Claude Tron Petit. Secretaria: Cristina Fuentes Macías. El criterio no es de la Suprema Corte.)

Index

The numbers here refer to paragraph numbers.

Index

www.ingramcontent.com/pod-product-compliance
Lightning Source LLC
Chambersburg PA
CBHW071346230926
51846CB00002B/461
9789041192288